Food Safety

How to *really* make a difference in food manufacturing

Adrian Banger &
Dr. Philip Barlow

AuthorHouse™ UK Ltd.
500 Avebury Boulevard
Central Milton Keynes, MK9 2BE
www.authorhouse.co.uk
Phone: 08001974150

First published by AuthorHouse 10/14/2009

ISBN: 978-1-4490-1016-4 (sc)

This book is printed on acid-free paper.

Acknowledgements

My heartfelt thanks go to all those people who have enriched my life by stimulating me to explore new ways of thinking and to take charge of my responses to the events around me.

The teachings of Wayne Dyer and Robert Dilts have been particularly instrumental in helping me develop the understandings and skills that enable me to effectively coach others.

The support and forbearance of my family, friends and colleagues has been greatly appreciated as I seek to live the concepts that I espouse.

Adrian Banger

It is hard to recognise all the people who have contributed to my knowledge over the years. Not only the tutors and work colleagues but the numerous students I have had the privilege to help with their learning have all taught me so much. It is to all these people that I give my thanks and which have all contributed to make me what I am today.

I have increasingly recognised that technical knowledge is not sufficient to be a good manger or tutor but it is also always necessary to consider the person/persons that you are trying to influence.

My family (and especially my late wife Jill) have always given me their support and encouragement to pursue my ideas and it is through them that I have been able to develop my approach to stimulate other people to achieve their goals.

Philip Barlow

Contents

Introduction

Food safety is just as much a people problem as it is a food science and technology issue. The majority of food safety problems occur not because food producers or handlers do not know how to prevent them but because for some reason non-compliance with the recognised procedures or practices occur. The consequences of knowledge not being applied are well publicised and have a major impact on those people concerned, with consumers dying through infected meats, major brands having to spend millions of pounds on product recalls and some companies actually going out of business as a result of a disastrous food safety incident.

> *"If you trace any problem back far enough you will eventually find people's attitudes and behaviours at its cause."*
>
> *Judy Suiter*

There is a wealth of information published in books, pamphlets and procedures on the technical aspects of food safety, there is an even greater volume of information about communication, managing and leading people and implementing change but few, if any, that bring these subjects together. This book seeks to redress that gap with specific guidance on approaches to facilitate behaviour change within the context of good food manufacturing practice.

Story telling has been recognised for millennia as the most effective way of sharing information in such a way that it influences people's lives. This book addresses major food safety issues through the way in which the central character, Tom Cunningham, a newly appointed Group Technical Manager, goes about dealing with them and provides a framework for developing the 'soft skills' necessary to enable sustainable behavioural change. There is specific guidance as to the approaches which can help the organisation embody best food safety practice at all levels.

> **"It's not what you know, but what you do with what you know, that makes the difference!"**

Whilst we are all unique we do share many common traits and many of the models for understanding both the commonalities and complexities of the human personality have been around for centuries. Hippocrates discovered that human behaviour could be usefully classified into four types and we shall be using a comparable four vector model to understand both the natural strengths and struggles of each behavioural style and the ways of communication that enable shared and better understanding.

> **"If the Golden Rule is to speak to others as *you* would like to be spoken to . . . then the Platinum Rule is to speak to others as *they* would like to be spoken to."**

In this book Tom learns how to recognise the four basic styles and adapt his approach to suit the style of the recipient, dramatically increasing the effectiveness of his communication and enhancing his personal credibility and trust across the company. Much of his time is spent seeking to influence Eric, the Works Manager, who has a highly directive and confrontational style. Most production or works managers demonstrate elements of this style and the ability of a technical manager to productively manage this relationship is fundamental to their ability to influence working practices in manufacturing.

Having enhanced his ability to communicate effectively, Tom moves on to discover the secrets of effective change management benefiting both from an understanding that to change behaviour he has to change the beliefs and values of all the people in the organisation and work to get their personal desires aligned with those of the company.

He also finds out why so many change initiatives fail to produce the results that were used to justify embarking on the project in the first place and gains knowledge and experience of the strategies for managing change that stack the odds in favour of achieving the initial objective. As he develops his ability to lead his team and influence the behaviour of the whole organisation he comes to understand the power of helping others develop new ways of thinking, in particular the maxim:

Ready, fire, aim

He realises that not only must he prepare for the changes he wishes to introduce to the company and take action, but also that it is necessary to put in place control systems that will enable him to track whether these actions are delivering the desired results.

At the end of his journey he reflects that his success in helping his company achieve the highest standards of food safety lay not only in his and their knowledge of what is required but in his ability to inspire everybody in the organisation to live and continuously develop best practice.

Getting the most out of this book

This book is designed to stimulate greater awareness of ways of influencing people and enabling long term behavioural change at the individual, team and organisational level.

You may already be familiar with some aspects of the areas covered and some may be totally new to you.

Whilst we all have our own individual learning styles, the more we can actively engage different parts of the brain, the more likely we shall be able to access that knowledge later on. At a minimum, if a message strikes a chord, it will take a few seconds for you to become aware of what it means to you. This process builds awareness, and awareness brings change and growth - automatically!

Many people find it beneficial to their learning to highlight or underline key phrases or write notes in the margin. There is some space at the rear of the book to record your key **insights**, reflect upon their **implications** and define your **intentions (3i's)**. If you prefer to keep your book pristine then do consider creating a learning log to record your insights and 'Aha moments'. The 3i format has proven to be a very effective format for helping translate awareness into action.

One Aha moment that I (Adrian) had many years ago was the significance of the acronym R2A2. It was around the time when the film 'Star Wars'

 =

Recognise
Relate
Assimilate
Act

popularised R2D2 and hence, by association, it was always easy to remember. I have since shared it at the start of all my courses as it sums up a simple but effective way of enhancing the value of learning.

The more we can relate information that we recognise to existing knowledge, the more we can assimilate it into our conscious awareness, and the more able we are to act upon it.

> **"Everyone stumbles over the truth from time to time, but most people pick themselves up and hurry off as though nothing ever happened."**
>
> *Sir Winston Churchill*

Chapter 1

Day 1 - Starting out

It was a grey autumn morning. A biting wind blew straight off the North Sea driving the rain almost horizontally as Tom drove through the gates of Regal Foods to start his new job.

In contrast to the weather outside, Tom felt most spring-like inside, with a sense of eager anticipation of the challenges ahead in his first role as Company Technical Manager. Since graduating with a degree in food science some 10 years earlier, Tom had held a variety of roles in food manufacturing and viewed this latest appointment as a, great opportunity to really make a difference to a major company whose reputation, in recent years, had had its ups and downs.

Tom had been attracted to join Regal Foods by an article he had read in one of the trade journals written by Roger Connor, the newly appointed Group MD, about his vision for the group to be recognised not just for the quality of its products and facilities but also for being a great place to work. He had been impressed by the openness with which Roger had recognised that achieving his vision was a lifetime journey, not a quick fix and that there was, and would be, at times, a substantial gap between his vision and current practices. He was also reassured by Roger's public commitment to develop the attitudes and skills at all levels within the organisation to close that gap.

This approach was in sharp contrast to his previous employer. There, the vision and values statements had been launched with a major fanfare after the board had gone on a five day retreat to Marbella with some highly paid consultants, yet no attempt was made to engage the rest of the company and explore their significance for the day to day operation.

Tom shuddered when he remembered the response he got when he challenged a decision to "re date" some production when a customer cut back their order at short notice. He recalled that he was not thanked for querying with the General Manager how that decision fitted with the published value "We will operate with integrity and an open style".

Regal Foods was primarily a manufacturer of quiches and supplied many of the major supermarket chains under their own labels. Tom had had some experience of the challenges involved when dealing with the different, and sometimes conflicting, demands of supermarket technologists and knew that his skills in diplomacy would sometimes be more important than his knowledge of food science. However, Tom was excited at the challenge especially as the company had recently acquired a vegetable processing factory some 35 miles away, in the heart of the Lincolnshire Wolds.

Although Tom had previously worked in a high risk environment producing cooked meats, he had no experience of the more basic standards associated with processing fresh vegetables.

Tom signed in at security and was directed to the office block where Ian Stuart, the Site Director, would be waiting to greet him. The site was much larger than he had been used to and had two main factory buildings, one he judged to be 30 or 40 years old, the other relatively new. He parked outside the office block and went in to meet Ian.

Tom had met Ian twice before during the selection procedure and he knew a little of Ian's background. Ian was in his mid fifties and was an accountant by profession. He had been General Manager for the previous owners before the company had been taken over by Regal Foods five years before. Ian welcomed Tom warmly and led him into his office; Tom looked around at the cream walls, polished wooden floor and the big, dark oak table that dominated the room. There was a traditional desk and filing cabinet at the far end; everything was very neat and tidy. Tom smiled inwardly as he recalled his last office and his filing system which had more to do with location of pile and depth than any normal filing system.

Tom sat down and gratefully accepted a cup of tea and a biscuit; it had been an early start that morning. Ian outlined the induction planned for Tom. First he would take him on a tour of the factory and introduce him to the other members of the management team and let him settle into his office. Half day slots had been booked with each of his key colleagues so that Tom could begin to understand their roles on site and Thursday was to be spent at the vegetable processing factory.

Ian then remarked with a smile "The best way to learn is by doing – so I would like you to take operational responsibility from the start of next week!" Tom thought to himself that this was certainly different from many of his previous job inductions where he spent weeks shadowing colleagues much to their, and his, frustration. Tom knew from past experience how much reading was required to familiarise himself with product specifications and manufacturing procedures. He was very conscious that even over his relatively short time in the food industry how much the volume of paperwork had grown and how easy it was to have documentation that was at odds with what actually happened.

Ian took Tom down to the laundry store and kitted him out with a set of white coats and a pair of white wellington boots. Ian pointed out that white coats with the green lapels were for general wear around the factory while those for use in the high risk area had red lapels and did not leave that area except for laundry.

Tom was pleased to see that they had ordered him a set of coats with his name on. This would certainly make it easier for him to get to know everybody by name if they also wore labelled overalls. Tom knew from past experience how simple things, such as addressing someone by name, helped to build effective relationships. Many of his colleagues in the past had not taken the time or trouble to learn the names of operatives and had been less effective managers as a result.

Tom recalled the time when he was faced with consistent small shortages of stock while working as warehouse manager. After many weeks of searching for explanations, one of the drivers suggested that he double check some of the loads awaiting despatch and there was the explanation! Drivers who got back early were often used to help make up loads and one driver would put extra cases on his load to sell or trade with other drivers at lorry parks. Tom knew that without the trusting relationship he had built with the majority of his team he could still be chasing those stock anomalies.

Tom's mind was brought back sharply to the present by Ian saying "Come and meet Eric, the Works Manager who looks after production and associated services." Eric said a curt "hello" and then started to tell Ian about a production problem. Tom stood patiently to one side observing the interaction between Ian and Eric. He had always enjoyed people watching and had been consciously working on his people reading skills. Eric was becoming quite agitated and was very explicit in laying the blame for the problem on a couple of people and wanted to formally discipline them. Tom pondered on whether this was one of the gaps that the MD had referred to in his article as Eric's behaviour was certainly at odds with having a learning not a blame culture!

After a while, Eric shot off and Tom asked "Does Eric always approach problems in that way? "Afraid so" said Ian "He is very good at getting things done but he does ruffle a few feathers at times." Tom wondered whether that might be an understatement. Time would tell.

Ian then took Tom across the yard to the main entrance of the factory and the standard risk changing area. Leaving their shoes to one side they sat down on the dividing bench, swung their legs over and put on their white wellingtons and coats. Ian passed Tom a green disposable hat and a green face mask to cover Tom's moustache. As they stopped at the hand sanitising station to wash their hands, Tom noticed a large stainless steel mirror adjacent to the exit with a sign above 'Are you properly dressed?' and two large pictures, one with a big tick and one with a big red cross. Ian explained that they had learned over the years how important it was to use visual reminders, particularly as more and more of their staff did not have English as their first language.

Ian led Tom down the corridor and into the technical department to meet Andrew, the Quality Manager. Andrew was busy looking at some analytical results with one of the laboratory technicians but broke away to greet Tom with a cool but not unfriendly smile. "Tom, this is Andrew" Ian continued, "Andrew has been with us for the last three years and has done some great work updating our systems – no doubt he will tell you all about them when you get together tomorrow morning."

Ian took Tom through the laboratory to an office at the end. "This is where you will be based" said Ian "and Andrew has his office next door". Tom looked around the office with its bare grey walls and functional desk and chair and thought about the changes needed to make it a more effective environment in which to work. I'll need a large white board for a start, he thought, recognising how he liked to think and plan in pictures, plus a couple of low chairs in the corner for more relaxed discussions.

Tom remembered the impact of an article he had read about how the layout of the room could affect the quality of communication. He recalled how much more productive it was to sit side by side, rather than face to face across a desk, when seeking to resolve contentious issues. Also, he recalled what a difference it had made when he had a major argument with Fred, the factory manager at his last company, about the most appropriate course of action to deal with some out of specification project. Tom had defined the problem on the board, put his proposed course of action and bullet point reasons underneath and then invited Fred to do the same. Tom and Fred had then sat down side by side and debated the pros and cons of each solution, putting any relevant new points on the board. After 10 minutes they had agreed a new course of action which satisfied them both. Tom reflected how different it had felt from the usual adversarial style of argument when one side invariably won at the expense of the other.

Ian then said to Tom "Come on, I will show you round the factory and let you get a feel for the challenges we have. Let's start with goods-in and then follow the flow through the production areas." They set off down the corridor back to the yard and round to the front of the older factory to the goods inwards bay. As they climbed the steps to the loading bay Tom noted that it was open to the elements and a couple of birds were perched on the rafters. Ian saw Tom looking up and said "The birds are a real pest, we do what we can to get rid of them but they keep coming back."

At that moment a Regal Foods truck arrived and the driver jumped out. Ian took Tom over and introduced him. "Tom, this is John. He works at the veg factory and comes up here three or four times a day with all our prepared vegetables." Tom smiled and said "Hi", noting quietly to himself that John's dress seemed more appropriate to the farmyard rather than a food factory.

John started to unload the plastic bins of diced onions onto a pallet ready for transfer into the chill store. As he did so, Tom noticed that some of the bins had suffered damage, with a couple of rims badly cracked. Another source of foreign bodies, he thought, especially as the bins were white and small pieces of plastic could easily get lost within the mass of diced onion. The potential for contamination was even higher as the onions appeared to have been diced directly into the bin and were only protected by a loose sheet of blue plastic. He made a mental note to review foreign body control procedures at both factories.

Ian then took Tom into the raw material chill. Tom was immediately struck by how congested it was. "How do you manage stock rotation?" he asked Ian. Ian pointed to the labels attached to each pallet. "We record date, quantity, product and supplier details on a label for each pallet", he replied.

Tom looked around and whilst labels were visible for many of the pallets, some did not appear to be labelled. "What about those part pallets over there?" he asked. Ian called Derek, the raw material intake supervisor, over, introduced him and then posed the same question. They went to the pallets to investigate but could not see any labels.

"I know they were labelled" said Derek, "I put them on myself. Hang on, let me get a hand barrow and pull them out." Derek pulled the first one out and sure enough there was a label, but it had been facing the wall. Derek pulled the second one out but there was not a label to be seen. He looked puzzled. "I know there was one, but they do occasionally fall off" he explained apologetically to Ian. "We've had much more of a problem since we introduced plastic pallets and stopped using staple guns. In the old days we used to staple the cards to the pallets and they rarely fell off."

Typical, thought Tom, solve one problem and create another! In eradicating wooden pallets and staples they had got rid of a major source of foreign bodies, but had compromised stock rotation and traceability of ingredients! Another challenge to deal with, he thought, I wish I had brought my notebook with me.

The three of them left the chill store and went into the dry goods area. Fortunately the store was less congested as it used the full height of the building for three pallet high racking. Tom noted that many of the products were stored on wooden pallets, some of which had suffered damage. He looked quizzically at Ian. Ian explained that ingredients came in from all over the world so it was not possible to specify plastic pallets as was the case for chilled raw materials. "However," explained Ian, "we have just completed our deboxing room where we decant all of our ingredients into our own plastic tubs before they go into the production area. Let's go have a look."

Ian led the way through the double doors at the end of the ingredient store. As Tom entered the well lit room he noticed the dividing wall with glazed panels and a plastic strip curtained doorway. Ian explained that the other side handled the fresh ingredients which required chill temperatures while this side all the dry ingredients were decanted. Ian pointed out the sieve and said what an impact it had had on their foreign body complaints. "Before we built this facility we used to get regular complaints about pieces of paper and string which had dropped into the sauce mixers when we slit the bags of starch. We have now eliminated this and have been able to screen out some other items which have been found in other dry powders. We used to have no idea where some of the items returned to us had come from, but now we know our dry ingredients are foreign body free."

Ian then took Tom through the curtained doorway into the chill area. "We have also made great strides here" he said. "We used to allow the boxes of tomatoes and fruit into the cooking area. Now, everything is decanted, inspected and transferred into our own bins. We have managed to totally eliminate cardboard from the mixing area of the factory."

Ian caught Tom looking through the window into the factory with a puzzled expression. "What's up, Tom?" asked Ian. "How do you get into the mixing area?" "Ah" said Ian "that was another of our big leaps forward. We now have just one pedestrian entrance into the mixing area through the hand wash area. In that way we have much better control over who goes in and the hand wash discipline. **We have learnt to use design to reinforce good practice.**" Tom was impressed, he remembered what a constant battle it had been in his previous factory to stop people wandering into the processing areas without washing and sanitising their hands.

Ian then took Tom round the corner into the bakery. They stopped at the hygiene station to wash their boots and sanitise their hands before entering the process hall. It was a large open space with high ceilings. The pastry mixers were in one corner and the forming and filling lines ran down the centre to the end, which was dominated by two large continuous ovens.

Tom looked up at all the services running overhead and mentally made a note to check the effectiveness of the cleaning procedures. A shiver of concern ran through him as he recalled reading about a factory decimated some years earlier by an explosion linked to dust build up on overhead structures. He would certainly spend some time with the night hygiene crews seeing what they actually did. He recalled being caught out in one of his earlier factories by a substantial difference between what the procedure said and what actually happened. That had been a very powerful learning experience for him and he was determined in his new job to engage all the staff in the development and documentation of key operating procedures rather than prepare them himself and then try to tell and sell them to the staff.

He recalled with a grimace, how he had worked so hard to create a suite of cleaning procedures in his last company, making sure that he had them all cross referenced to the HACCP scheme and integrated into his document control system. He had then spent hours training the hygiene crew, working nights and weekends to ensure that they all knew what was required of them only to find that when the internal audit took place some three months later many of the operatives had reverted back to the old ways of working. It was a salutary lesson in the consequences of not harnessing the hearts and minds of the actual 'doers'.

"Penny for your thoughts." Tom was suddenly aware of Ian speaking. Tom blushed and apologised. "Sorry Ian Looking up and seeing the potential for dust on the overheads not only to be a source of foreign body contamination, but also a potential safety issue reminded me of my embarrassment in my last job when I was caught out by the very internal audit system that I had set up! I had created procedures, communicated them carefully and then naively expected them to be followed."

Ian smiled and said "I am sure you will find plenty of opportunities to improve the way in which we do things here. Eric, in particular, has yet to grasp **that deciding what needs to change and issuing instructions rarely leads to his staff consistently doing what he wants. I fear the more directive he becomes and tries to force compliance, the less effective he is in building the attitudes to quality that we all seek.** It will certainly help us work better as a management team if you can help Eric to use his willingness to confront more sparingly."

With that, Ian took Tom over and showed him the three production lines. Ian explained that these lines were used to produce all the savoury quiches and the cases for the patisserie range which they were shortly starting to produce in their new factory next door. "You have come at an exciting time," Ian remarked, "we have won the contract to produce a new range of patisserie under the St Marcus brand and you know how demanding they can be."

"Sure do," said Tom, "we launched a range for St Marcus in my last company and the technologists almost lived on site during the early days. It was certainly a challenging time, creating specifications and documenting procedures while still getting on with my day job. Fortunately, I had a great number two, with a fine eye for detail, and happy to work alone, which left me time to spend with the plant operators and technologists."

"I certainly used all my skills in building relationships then," said Tom. "Many a time the operators would come to me and warn me of the possible unforeseen consequences of the decisions I had taken."

"I really came to appreciate the value of the deposits that I had made into the 'emotional bank account' as Steven Covey calls it, with the guys on the shop floor. I recall my first job straight after university. My ability to form open, trusting relationships was much more important in enabling me to succeed than any knowledge I had gained from my degree."

Ian nodded in agreement, quietly reflecting to himself how pleased he was to have someone on his team to balance the "hang them first, ask questions later" style of Eric, his Works Manager. Sure, Eric got things done and had been very successful in shaking up the complacency that he had inherited, but the consequences were starting to show and operators were burying problems in an attempt to avoid the wrath of Eric so that when they did eventually surface they were much more difficult to resolve.

As they walked down the line Tom noticed some examples of temporary engineering, with product guides being taped into position with gaffer tape which was starting to fray – another source of potential foreign bodies, he thought. Ian noticed Tom looking and explained that Dick, the engineer, was great at fixing problems but had trouble negotiating with Eric to have access to the line to install a properly engineered solution, especially as the main customer had recently re-launched their quiche range with new varieties and volumes which were currently running 50% over plan.

Tom immediately recognised the gap between the public commitment of the Group MD to be recognised for the quality of their products and facilities and actual operating practices. He resolved to make a note as soon as he got back into the office. He remembered what good advice he had received from his previous boss on his first day. "Tom, always carry a notebook and record everything that does not immediately make sense to you. Then review those points once you have been here for three months – fresh pair of eyes and all that." Tom reflected upon how useful that had been, how reviewing his early notes had reminded him of areas where there could be improvements to current practices but which no longer registered with him as he saw them every day.

They moved on down the line to the entrance to the ovens and stood watching the filled quiches being automatically marshalled into event lines on the intake belt. This was the first time that Tom had seen continuous belt baking ovens and was keen to find out more. Ian explained that the ovens could bake 2,500 quiches an hour and that they worked continuously from Sunday night until Saturday morning as they took so long to get up to temperature and cool down. Ian noted with relief that the opening to the oven was only about 150mm high, remembering with a shudder how two engineers had been killed after being sent into a similar style of oven to repair a fault without the oven being given proper time to cool down. Given Eric's focus on maximising production, Tom was relieved to see that there was no danger of any similar shortcuts being taken here.

Ian pointed out the door by the side of the oven and explained how fitting it with an emergency only lock had really helped the discipline of rigidly separating staff working in the high risk, cooked product packing areas from those who worked in the rest of the factory. Ian led the way back out of the pastry and filling section and along to the changing area where they had come in. They hung their coats up, binned their hats and sat down on the bench to remove their boots. Tom looked around him. Some of the lockers had seen better days, with doors bent and rust starting to show through. Ian noticed Tom looking at the lockers and said apologetically "Those lockers are only three years old, but people do not treat them with respect. They were damaged within weeks of being installed."

Tom recalled reading an article about how upgrading the environment rarely leads to improved behaviour without a change in what people value and their beliefs about themselves. He made a mental note to find the article and refresh his memory. He had a strong sense of knowing that this could be highly relevant to his desire to help build the quality culture described in the article by the Group MD.

They put their shoes on and made their way along the corridor to the high risk changing area which was similarly laid out with the bench across the middle, only this time the coats had red collars and the hats and snoods were also red. Ian selected a pair of white clogs for Tom, explaining that they kept a pool of clogs just for use in the high risk area. Noticing a quizzical look on Tom's face, Ian reassured him that they were regularly sanitised so he wouldn't come to any harm!

They made their way to the hand wash station and went through the normal routine of washing, scrubbing, drying and finishing with an alcohol rinse. Ian proudly pointed out the new red floor; he explained this was made of a special soft compound which cleaned the underside of the shoes.

They walked around the exit of the oven and Ian introduced Tom to Moira, one of his Q A team. She was busy checking the internal temperature of the quiches as they came out of the oven. Tom noticed a 'critical control point' sign above the conveyor. Ian explained that one of the operatives on their HACCP team had suggested putting the signs up. It was not something that Tom had done in his previous factory, but he could see the benefit in building more general awareness of the importance of understanding the HACCP schedules for all the processes. The quiches were marshalled onto a plastic slatted conveyor belt for transfer into the blast chiller.

Tom smiled to himself as he noted that he had not yet seen any rubber conveyor belts in the factory. They had been a real bane of his previous life, both from a hygiene and foreign body perspective. He had never been able to find conveyors where the design allowed for easy access under the belt and kept the belt on track. It had been a constant battle to stop frayed edges becoming a source of foreign body complaints.

Ian then took Tom up the stairs to the packing mezzanine where the quiches exited the chiller and were packed into their individual cartons. He stood silently watching the operation for a few minutes, mentally noting the areas of vulnerability. The packed quiches then disappeared through a hole in the wall and he could observe through the glazed panel operatives palletising the product. Ian remarked that Tom could explore that part of the process later once they had changed back into their standard risk clothing.

As they were coming back down the stairs, Ian glanced up at the clock on the wall opposite. "Is that the time?" he exclaimed. "My stomach tells me it is time for lunch. Come on, I will show you the canteen."

The canteen was housed in the rear of the old factory and had obviously seen better days. It was cramped, the furniture was scruffy and the floor was worn. However, the walls and ceiling appeared to be freshly painted. Tom looked up and noticed that the diffusers around the lights were clean and in good repair, a positive sign he thought. He had learned that the state of the light fittings, and the cleanliness of the fire extinguishers, were often good indicators of the rigour of a hygiene system. When he had audited some of his supplier factories in the past, he had got the impression that they had had a superficial clean in honour of his visit, but often ignored more difficult to reach or non production items.

Ian noticed Tom looking around and explained that he had been fighting for some time to extend and refurbish the canteen but he had never been able to get approval from the Board. However, he hoped that the appointment of Roger Connor as the new Group MD would lead to the project being sanctioned.

Tom agreed that the current facility was not in keeping with the values espoused by Roger and his commitment to making the company one of the best places to work. Tom thought back to his first job after university when he had joined a small privately owned company as Quality Manager. The owner had spoken eloquently about his commitment to quality and the way in which he valued the people who worked for him. He recalled with a wry smile the glossy mission and values statement that had greeted him when he entered reception and his disillusionment when he saw the contrast between the luxury of the owner's office with its thick pile carpets, expensive designer furniture and original works of art on the walls and the state of the canteen and cloakrooms with their tatty plastic furniture, bent and broken lockers and floors which had seen their last coat of paint many years before. He remembered it becoming evident over the following months how little credibility the owner had with people on the shop floor and the impact this had had on his effectiveness in leading the company.

> **Leadership credibility is determined more by the nature and consistency of your actions than the eloquence of your words.**

This experience had really embedded deep within his psyche the importance of 'walking your talk'. Tom reflected that time had really been a powerful learning experience for him and had led him to regularly take time out to reflect upon how good he was at actually living and doing what he said was important.

Tom was still lost in his thoughts when he heard Ian's voice. "You seem deep in thought, care to share them?" asked Ian.

Tom smiled. "I was thinking back to my first job and the contrast between the MD's office and the works canteen and how that undermined his declared statement that "the Company's greatest asset was its employees". It really brought home to me how perceptive people on the shop floor are when it comes to the foibles of senior management. I often say "People on the shop floor can smell bullsh*t at a hundred yards." Ian laughed, "You are so right!"

They soon finished lunch and Ian announced that he needed to go to a meeting, so would Tom like to spend the afternoon exploring the information currently produced by his department. "I know you are not due to be with Andrew until tomorrow morning, but I am sure he will be happy to talk you through the systems this afternoon. Are you OK to find your way back?"

Tom nodded and got up. He was very conscious that he preferred interacting with people, rather than working by himself doing paperwork. However, he recognised that accurate, comprehensive documentation was an essential element of being a top class food producer. "No time like the present" he said quietly to himself and headed off down the corridor in the direction of his office.

Tom sat down behind his desk and surveyed his new surroundings. Very basic was a fair description! He closed his eyes and began to visualise what would need to change so that it became a warm, inviting but productive environment that would both encourage people to come and chat with him and at the same time convey a professional image. He recognised how important it was to be consistent in the messages he was sending out, even when he wasn't saying anything.

He recalled his thoughts from earlier that morning, white boards were certainly a priority – could he be cheeky and ask for one of those new electronic whiteboards he had seen on one of his visits to a supplier? Being able to capture and reproduce the information on the board had certainly made the meeting more productive. Nothing ventured, nothing gained, he thought, I must research the options. He then turned his attention to the far corner, a great space for three chairs and a low table to create a more relaxed environment for discussing issues - or would I be better to get a table and chairs so that we could hold meetings here? Better check out if there are any meeting rooms for general use, he thought.

At that point there was a knock on his door. It was Andrew. "Welcome aboard" Andrew said with a smile and approached Tom, arm outstretched. It was a warm and friendly handshake, not the bone crushing power shake favoured by one of his previous colleagues.

"Pull up a chair," Tom invited "tell me about the department, what is working well and what do we need to be concerned about?"

Andrew sat back in his chair and thought for a while before speaking. "Well", he said "on the plus side I have been able to get most of the procedures documented and the specifications are reasonably up to date. However, I do have a constant battle with the production staff to complete their records accurately and hand them in at the end of the shift."

"What have you done about it?" asked Tom. "Well, I keep raising it in the weekly operations meeting. Eric gets uptight and goes and gives the supervisors a good telling off, things improve for a couple of days and then they drift back to where they have always been; key data are not fully completed and record sheets are left lying around the factory rather than being brought back to us for checking and filing."

Tom was tempted to jump in with some suggestions as to what they might do differently, but he had learned that it was more productive to explore further and try and tease out some options from Andrew before offering up his own suggestions. He had been reading a book on coaching skills that weekend and remembered how important it was not to take ownership of the solution away from the person being coached.

"What could you do differently?" enquired Tom with a smile. "A wise old ex colleague of mine always used to say:

a good definition of insanity is doing the same thing and expecting a different result!"

Andrew laughed and said "I guess I have been guilty of that on a number of occasions. Eric hauling them in and telling them to improve obviously doesn't work. In fact, I overheard some comments from a couple who had been to one of his meetings that the more angry and vocal he became the more people became defensive and turned off and the less was actually achieved."

"Given that that doesn't work, how might you get people to complete all the forms and hand them in?" Tom queried.

"Well" said Andrew, "I could set up a meeting with the key operatives and explain why the information was so important, how we needed complete and accurate records to pass our BRC audit . . . perhaps I could devise a system for checking the forms?"

"That could certainly help" Tom reflected. "If people understood not only what to do but why it needs doing, they would certainly be more likely to do it. However:

getting people to understand what needs to be done is relatively easy. Getting them to consistently do it is a major challenge!"

Tom pulled over a sheet of paper and started drawing; he divided the paper up into four squares explaining that he had recently read a book about the impact of actively engaging people with the performance of the company. One model really stuck out in his mind. In one square he put 'telling', in the next 'selling', in the one underneath 'inclusion' and 'co-creation' in the last. He explained that the 'co – creation' box was where the leader defined the objective and then facilitated the group to come up with their own solutions.

Tom passed the piece of paper over to Andrew and asked him to rank the boxes according to how much ownership the individuals involved might feel for the solutions. Andrew paused and then said 'telling' would be the lowest, then 'selling' followed by 'inclusion' with 'co-creation' the highest. "And what might the order be if we were looking for long term behaviour change?" asked Tom. "Well the same, I guess" replied Andrew.

"Exactly" replied Tom. "Let's see if I can remember how John Smythe described the outcomes in his book.[1] He says that the typical outcome for the 'telling' approach is to create 'Hooligans and Spectators'. That really struck home for me when I thought back to when I had just been told to do something without understanding the reason or having any say in the way it was to be done.

He uses the term 'compliant collaborators' for the 'selling', 'willing collaborators' for the 'inclusion' and 'personally committed reformers' as the outcome from using the 'co-creation' approach.

Andrew was quiet for a moment as the significance of the model began to sink in. Tom could almost hear the cogs whirring as Andrew thought through how this could be used to help resolve the problem in hand.

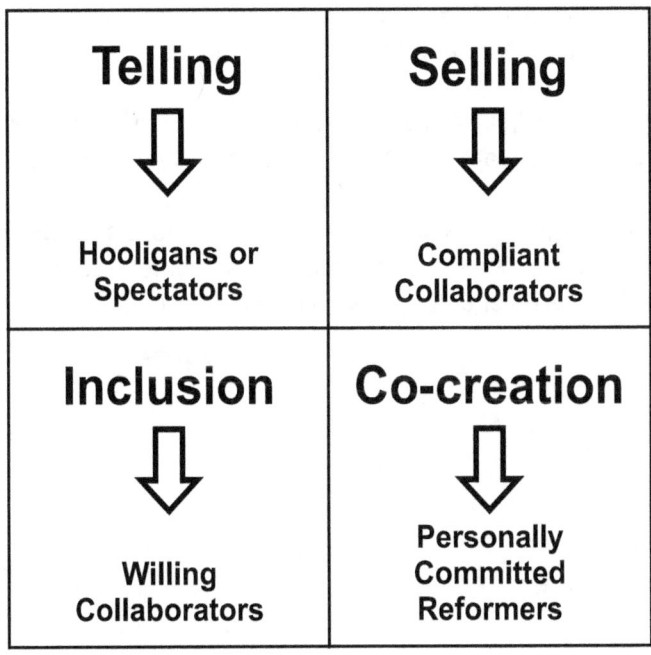

"Now I understand why Eric's approach hasn't worked!" exclaimed Andrew. "Maybe if I got a few of the key people together, explained the problem and invited them to come up with ideas as to how to solve it, we might make progress?"

"Exactly" said Tom. "Just imagine how differently they will feel if they understand why it is so important to have accurate and complete records and are encouraged to work out for themselves what changes to the procedures will help achieve the objective. Remember though, you still have an important role in the process to support them and help them check out the impact of their solutions on the rest of the quality system."

> **"If the people whose behaviour creates the problem have ownership of the solution, then you are much more likely to get lasting behaviour change."**

"Thanks for that," said Andrew "I think I know who would be best to ask I will talk to them in the morning and see when we could set up a meeting."

"Do make sure that you talk to Eric first," warned Tom, "it is going to be your project, but it is better to have Eric on board, even though he may not be actually involved in any of the meetings, rather than have him feel that things are going on in his area that he doesn't know about.

I think it would be helpful if you could take me through the key elements of the quality system so that I can start to understand how you do things here."

An intense two hours of discussion followed, until Tom announced, "I think we are getting to the point of information overload. Let's call it a day and I will go and find the hotel that Ian has organised for me."

Chapter 2

Day 1 – Evening

Tom found the hotel quite easily. It was a small country house hotel about five miles from the factory. He parked his car and walked to the front of the hotel. A bell tinkled as he opened the door. Almost immediately a man appeared from out the back.

"Welcome to Marshbank" the man said, "I am Richard. Ian told me to expect you. I understand you are going to be staying with us for a few weeks while your house purchase goes through. I hope you will be comfortable here. I have put you in room one at the front, it is a good size and has a desk should you want to work in the evening. Dinner is served from 6.30 to 9 pm. If you get down early you will have choice of tables as most of our bookings are for 8 pm onwards. Come; let me show you to your room."

Richard led Tom up the stairs and opened the door to room one and gave Tom the key. "Just let me know if you need anything." With that Richard shut the door and left Tom to unpack.

A quick shower and change into more comfortable clothes and Tom was already feeling hungry. Ian had told Tom about his many happy experiences of dining at the Marshbank.

Tom was the first person in the restaurant and sat in the window, enjoying the view and taking the opportunity to reflect upon the day. He was pleased to have had an early opportunity to adopt a coaching approach with Andrew, knowing from past experience how important it was to lead by example. The rest of his team would almost certainly have quizzed Andrew about his afternoon with the new 'boss'.

After a short while, an older gentleman entered the restaurant and sat at the next table. He nodded "Good evening" and proceeded to study the menu.

Richard then came in to take the orders. "Tom, this is Walter. Walter is one of our long term regular guests, so you will often see him here. Walter, this is Tom. Tom has just joined Regal Foods and will be staying with us for the next few weeks until his house is ready.

What can I interest you in tonight? The salmon is very good; it was caught only last night." Tom and Walter both ordered the salmon and Richard left.

"What brings you to this part of the world?" Tom enquired. "Work" replied Walter, "I have been helping a packaging company near here for some months with a culture change project. The MD wants to develop a more empowered workforce and I have been working with him and the team for eighteen months now."

"That must be interesting work" remarked Tom. "Have you always been a consultant?"

"No" said Walter, "As a matter of fact I used to run food factories but now I say that I am paid to play! I am very fortunate to spend my working life coaching individuals and teams. I just love seeing the way people can develop when challenged and supported."

"What led you to make the change?" enquired Tom.

"Well" replied Walter, "it's a long story. I had worked for a number of major food producers in production and technical roles but had always fancied having a bigger role in a smaller organisation. Eventually I landed a job as Operations Manager (Director Designate) for a medium sized, privately owned company producing dry sauce mixes. I was the first professionally trained and experienced production person in the company's history. I knew nothing about dry powder blending or packing but I felt I did know about managing people and developing supportive systems. There were plenty of opportunities to make a difference. The management team that I inherited were largely keen and committed but had never had any real investment in their development so they tended to be doers rather than managers. Over five years I built up a good team and our unit costs of production fell quite substantially. However, I discovered that the owner was keener on debating the business concepts that he had read in the Harvard Business Review than in the practical realities of how to get the best out of a hundred or so people working in a manufacturing set up that had grown like topsy over the years. I was eventually made a director when the owner recruited a new marketing director. Unfortunately, the new marketing director was even more entranced by the conceptual side of business and we soon came to blows as he was the MD's protégé and they spoke the same language. My challenging of them both to think through the consequences of these 'new solutions' led to more and more tension and I was 'invited to find other job opportunities!'"

My next role was as Group Production Director for a fish company that had taken over two other companies, both based at least 200 miles away. My job was to integrate the operations of the three plants. Initially I got on well with the MD and made some progress in getting the systems right and recruiting a new team. However, the MD decided to merge the three separate company accounting systems into one consolidated set of accounts with a manufacturing division and a sales division, without any parallel running. Even though I did not know as much about managing change then as I do now, I knew it was a high risk strategy. Sure enough it was - we had no credible management accounts for three months and when some were eventually prepared it showed that manufacturing had lost £250,000 and sales had made £100,000. I can remember the MD's face when I queried how the costings had been derived; even though I was not an accountant I knew that the transfer price would determine the relative profitability of each division. I reminded him that according to the last costings, the Sales Director had been taking contracts at 12% margin and the typical labour cost was around 25% of ex factory cost. The factory had to work weekends to produce the products at premium rates, so it was no surprise that the company was operating at a loss.

Needless to say, our relationship went downhill from then on. I had a moment of realisation driving home one day that much as I enjoyed being a bigger fish in a smaller pond, I would never work for one owner again. So when the time came to part company I immediately set up my own consultancy.

Initially, I was primarily providing technical support to smaller food companies. But progressively I found that:

> **it was not lack of knowledge that held companies back but lack of the soft skills to develop a culture where people utilised their knowledge and were able to perform at their best.**

Tom was impressed with the openness with which Walter had shared his story and could quickly see that Walter could be a very useful sounding board during these early weeks as he started to make his mark at Regal Foods. The Universe works in mysterious ways, he said to himself.

"That's a fascinating story, Walter, I would love to find out more about your experiences, I am sure they can help me really make a difference at Regal" said Tom.

"Delighted to help in any way I can. Unfortunately, I have promised to meet an old colleague this evening and have to leave shortly. However, before I go let me ask you a question. Do you know how pearls are created?"

Tom thought for a moment and said "Isn't it something to do with a piece of sand irritating the oyster?"

"Absolutely right, but do you know why some oysters produce pearls and others do not?"

"No" said Tom, wondering where this conversation was going.

"Well" Walter explained "the key factor is the size of the sand particle. Too small and nothing happens, too large and it gets expelled. It has to be exactly the right size of irritant to produce a pearl. So if you want to produce 'pearls' at Regal make sure you challenge the system sufficiently to stimulate real pearls of progress, but not so much that it conspires to expel you! On that note, enjoy your evening. I will be staying here tomorrow night as well, so perhaps we can continue our conversations then."

Walter got up and left, leaving Tom to enjoy the last of the evening sunshine streaming through the window.

Tom wandered outside. The sun was still warm so he decided to go for a walk and explore the area down by the river. "Exercise and thinking time must be good" he silently said to himself as he walked down the drive and along the road towards a church he had spotted on his drive to the hotel.

As he walked he reflected on the day. There was certainly much to reflect upon. Some aspects of the factory were better than he recalled from his first sighting on the quick tour he had been given at his final interview. There were no surprises with Ian. Tom had judged him on his first meeting to be steady and reliable and nothing today had happened to call that judgement in to question. It was the first time he had met Andrew and Tom was delighted that he appeared to be so open to learning and hoped he would turn out to be a competent number two. Of all the people he had met he had the most concerns about Eric. Eric had not been particularly welcoming and Tom sensed that Eric had a strong sense of right and wrong. If you agreed with Eric you were right, if you disagreed, you were wrong!

Tom turned off the road, down the track towards the little church and the river, still deep in thought, reflecting upon his first day. From nowhere, he recalled an article he had read on the characteristics of top leaders. It talked about how:

> **as you became more senior in an organisation your effectiveness had more to do with your ability to influence others than your knowledge of the function that you were leading.**

With that thought in mind, Tom made his way slowly back to the hotel.

Chapter 3

Day 2

Tom awoke early, the autumn sun still having enough strength to light up the room. Such a different start compared with yesterday he reflected. He got up, showered and dressed and made his way down for an early breakfast. He was the first one into the dining room and Richard, the hotel owner, soon appeared and greeted him with a cheery "Good morning. What would you like for breakfast?"

Tom glanced at the menu and saw scrambled egg with smoked salmon on whole grain bread, indulgent and good for me! He thought.

"Scrambled egg with smoked salmon and Earl Grey tea please" he replied.

At that moment Walter walked in. Great morning" he said breezily. "It is indeed" replied Tom "Would you like to join me, I really enjoyed our conversation last night."

Walter sat down opposite him. "What have you got lined up for today?" he enquired.

"Well" said Tom, "I shall be completing my initial tour of the factory and then spending the rest of the day exploring the quality systems that Regal use. I am particularly interested to see how they approach HACCP; some companies seem to make it very complicated and bureaucratic."

"They certainly do" replied Walter. "Getting the right balance between documenting all key information, and not getting submerged in a sea of paper, can certainly be very challenging. I have frequently found that some simpler systems, that were obviously used and understood by everyone in manufacturing, were often much more effective in ensuring product quality than very detailed systems created by a quality specialist and imposed upon the production team. I look forward to hearing all about your experiences this evening. What time are you planning to eat tonight?"

"How about seven o'clock?" replied Tom as he got up from the table.

"I look forward to it, have an interesting day."

Tom went back to his room, collected his briefcase and made his way out to the car park. It was a short drive to the factory and Tom soon found himself at the security gate. He signed himself in and then drove to the office block to meet Ian.

"Morning Ian" said Tom, "what's in the programme for today?"

"Well, we can finish our tour of the main factory and then I thought we could explore the old factory which we are about to refurbish to take the new patisserie lines. Then, I thought you could meet up with Andrew to find out more about our quality systems before spending some time with Eric later this afternoon."

With that they both set off for the main factory. As they were about to enter, Eric came charging out, his face like thunder. "What's wrong?" asked Ian. "They cocked up again" he spluttered. "Supersave came on last night just as I was going home and cut back their order for the 7-inch cheese and tomato, but we already had some of the ingredients mixed so I sent the shift manager an email telling him to take an early meal break once they completed the order and switch to today's code on start up as it would be near enough to the 6pm changeover. We would then cut back on today's production, but they went ahead and coded all the production with yesterday's date. We've now got a pallet of product with yesterday's date and no orders for it! I'm going to give him what for when he comes on shift at two."

"Calm down, Eric. I will call the product manager at Supersave and agree how the extra pallet should be handled. I will let you know the result" said Ian.

Eric shot off back into the factory.

"Is it common practice to pre-code?" enquired Tom. "I recall my last company lost a big account just before I joined when a technologist discovered that they had been pre-coding production."

"We have really tightened up on it here over the last two years and we now have much stricter disciplines about how do deal with product over runs. Old habits die hard and Eric is still prone to wanting to bend the rules on occasions. His heart is in the right place in wanting to avoid waste, but he doesn't always think through the potential consequences of his actions" Ian said wearily.

Tom made a mental note to explore the mixes in progress and the coding issue with Andrew. I do hope they are not compounding the problem by fudging record sheets, he thought quietly to himself. I will find out more about it before I challenge Ian. Allowing this practice is certainly out of alignment with the MD's pronouncements on the vision and values of the company.

They made their way into the changing room and donned their protective clothing in silence, each lost in thought about the exchange with Eric.

"Let's skip the packing area and go direct to the new patisserie area" suggested Ian, "I would like to talk to Supersave sooner rather than later and get agreement on how best to handle the extra pallet."

They soon arrived in the old factory, which had been cleared of all its equipment and was now an empty shell."

"We have a great opportunity here" said Ian enthusiastically. "We can take this opportunity to show how much we are able to live the vision of being a world class food manufacturer. This is the first major project under Roger Connor's reign and I know from my conversations with him that he is determined it should embody his vision for the company."

"It is certainly a great opportunity" agreed Tom, "no doubt everyone will be watching how we proceed."

"Dick's in charge of the project from an engineering point of view" explained Ian, "but I want to make sure that we tap into as much expertise as we can to make sure we not only get the physical layout right but also get the people who are going to run the plant on board as well."

"How do you plan to do that?"

"I have been thinking about setting up a project team which would naturally include Dick, for engineering matters, Eric for production, and you for technical. I also propose to include a couple of our most experienced operators, plus specialist outsiders as appropriate. I am also considering asking St Marcus as to whether they would be prepared to second one of their technologists to the team."

"Wow, that certainly would be different to the projects I have previously been involved with" Tom reflected, "and it would really show that we were committed to engaging all the key players in the success of the new plant. We never went as far as that in my last company, but I do recall we got some real benefit from discussing the layout of a new line we were creating with the biologist from our pest control contractor. She was able to give us some valuable guidance on the locations of the UV light traps / exterminators so as to avoid attracting insects into the area and she had some good ideas about how to incorporate proofing into the design of the doors. This saved us a lot of money and we never really had a problem in that area with flying insects, even in the height of summer."

"We are also going to take the opportunity to put automatic data capture into each stage of the process so that we can not only monitor yields and throughputs but also capture key processing parameters as well. We are considering having all the operators book onto the line with magnetic swipe cards so that we will know exactly what our labour costs are. It will certainly be a very different way of working for everyone compared to the current operation," Ian explained enthusiastically. "I just hope we can get all the workers on the shop floor to buy into the changes."

"It often is a challenge" admitted Tom. "We had a major problem changing ways of working in my last plant. The management team were all convinced of the benefits, but for some reason the operators were reluctant to change and performance actually went down for a time before we eventually got them to understand that they would really benefit from the new working practices."

"Perhaps there are some lessons we could learn from your experiences to help us with this project."

"Delighted to help in any way I can," said Tom, knowing how much he liked to be involved with anything new.

"I had better go back to the office and phone Supersave and see whether I can pull in a favour and get them to accept that pallet. Hopefully the time I have invested in building a relationship with their buyer will pay off. You're scheduled to spend most of the day with Andrew and then be with Eric at four this afternoon, aren't you? Best of luck with Eric, he's not the easiest person to get on with. However, his bark is worse than his bite!" With that, Ian turned on his heels and headed back to his office.

Tom stood for a few moments collecting his thoughts. What approach would work the best with Eric? He wondered as he tried to recall how he had handled characters like Eric in the past.

Still deep in thought, Tom made his way back to the office to meet Andrew.

"Morning Andrew, how are you today?" he asked with a smile.

"OK, but frustrated with Eric trying to break the rules on coding again" replied Andrew wearily. "We sit in meetings and all agree that it is against our values, but he still does it."

"I'm due to meet Eric at four this afternoon; I will raise it with him and see what his response is. In the meantime, I would really like to start to understand where you are on HACCPs. I was responsible, particularly in the early days, for writing the HACCP schemes in my last company so I am interested in finding out what approach you use."

"Well" said Andrew, "we are in the process of changing our HACCP documentation. Like you, I created most of it in the early days and then sought to get it implemented and followed but it was always an uphill struggle to keep it up to date, particularly as we made changes to the plant and process. When I first started compiling them I used to create one HACCP plan for each product and record all the CCPs including such things as supplier approvals, hygiene procedures and waste management. I ended up creating a mountain of paper and it almost became a full-time job trying to ensure that we honoured the fundamental principle of:

say what we do and do what we say!

Last year I went on an advanced HACCP course and realised that much of the information I was putting into each HACCP scheme could be covered more generically. I also realised how much more effective we could be if we broadened the HACCP team from just management and included some of the plant operators.

Naturally, we had to train them in the basic principles of HACCPs and getting Eric's agreement to release them was a struggle. He would always claim they were too busy. Fortunately, I had great support from Ian and eventually I was able to set up a training schedule which was ultimately kept to!

I also took the opportunity to put our QA staff through the same training and now some of the documentation is created by members of the QA team in conjunction with the production operatives and then presented to the HACCP team for approval and sign off. It has certainly made my life a lot easier and we no longer have the same problems with getting the production staff to follow the procedures."

Tom was delighted at the news. It certainly sounded as if there was a good foundation upon which he could build.

"Who's on the HACCP team at the moment?"

"Currently, Ian leads it. Eric represents production, Dick engineering, me for QA and then we invite in an operator and a member the QA team from the area under discussion. Ian did say that he was hoping to pass over the responsibility for leading the team once you had established yourself."

Tom was pleased to hear that. It would give him a real opportunity to develop the systems that he wanted.

"Pretend I was an auditor from the British Retail Consortium (BRC) who has not visited the plant before and asks to be taken through your HACCP system."

"OK" said Andrew, "let's start with the Pre-requisites" and he pulled down the quality manual from the shelf. "As well as our general quality policies we also include in this manual such things as our supplier approval policy and procedures here, traceability and recall, and general quality procedures such as calibration of our measuring equipment and document control procedures."

While Tom was browsing through the quality manual, Andrew pulled down his hygiene manual.

"This covers all our hygiene policies and procedures, our record of training and our COSHH (Control of Substances Hazardous to Health) assessments for all the chemicals that we use on site."

Tom was pleased to see that the documents appeared to be well structured, with clear issue and amendment dates and written in plain English.

"You have obviously put a lot of work into these" he remarked.

"Yes" said Andrew, "it is important to me to have system and order and I am much more comfortable when I know everything is properly documented and up to date."

Tom smiled, "I think we will work together well as a team. Order and structure do not come naturally to me and I really have to consciously work at it. I know how important it is, but I often get so tied up talking with people that I don't allow sufficient time to complete all the paperwork that seems to go with the job these days!"

"Indulge me. Let's go out into the factory and meet the team, introduce me to all the QA team and the key operatives in production."

Two hours quickly flew by as Tom and Andrew went walkabout. Tom soon realised that he could not remember all their names but was comforted by the knowledge that he had the name tags on their overalls to fall back on. He remembered with a smile the embarrassment he had felt when a particularly well-endowed lady in his first company had misinterpreted his gaze as he sought to read her name label as an overt interest in her physical assets! Must be careful, he thought, I know my intentions but the other person will interpret my behaviour through the filter of their experiences and may come to a very different conclusion to that intended!

It was soon lunchtime and Tom took the opportunity to find out more about Andrew in a relaxed setting. Under Tom's gentle probing, Andrew began to open up about his views on life at Regal Foods, the activities and attitudes that energised him and those that did the opposite. Tom was delighted to find that whilst Andrew obviously had a different behavioural style to himself, they appeared to share similar values. They both valued honesty and integrity and believed their role as managers was to act as a guide for others in the organisation rather than play God. Tom was greatly reassured by their discussions for he had learned that:

> **a diversity of behavioural styles can enhance team performance providing there is mutual respect and clear communication, but a diversity of values will tear the team apart unless it is very carefully managed.**

Conscious of time, they went back into the office and Andrew continued to take Tom through their quality system.

It was soon four pm and Tom set off to find Eric. Eric's office was located high on the mezzanine floor with a good view of all the pastry making and filling lines beneath him.

Tom looked out of the window and noticed Eric busy working on one of the depositors. He noted wryly to himself that there appeared to be an operator standing by while Eric cleared the blockage. The line started up again and a short while later Eric appeared in the doorway.

"Sorry I'm late. The depositor was not working properly and that bloody operator was standing by and letting it deposit short weights. God knows how many rejects we would have had if I hadn't spotted it."

Tom smiled to himself as he recognised the "Action Man" syndrome. He had come to appreciate that certain people really thrive on fire-fighting and relished the opportunity to get directly involved at every possible opportunity. The advice of a more experienced manager who had become his mentor in his first job after university came flooding back.

> **'Balance is everything, get directly involved and lead from the front on occasions, but do *not* let others become dependent upon you to solve their problems.'**

Eric sat down in front of Tom and immediately challenged him with the question "What are you going to do to improve quality and get our costs down?"

Tom was initially taken aback by such a confrontational approach and was struggling to find a way to answer that did not sound defensive or patronising.

Suddenly, one of the line supervisors burst in with a message that the gluer on the carton line wasn't working. Eric leapt to his feet and with barely a backwards glance said "Sorry, must go, let's catch up tomorrow" and disappeared out of the office, with the supervisor hard on his heels.

Tom sat quietly for a few moments, gathering his thoughts. How do I get across to Eric how out of alignment his behaviour is with the values published by Roger Connor? How can we build a workforce that is empowered and happily applies their knowledge and intellect to helping the company move forward when one of the key managers insists on being Mr Fix-it and the sole source of solutions?

The words of Ghandi suddenly sprang to mind:

> '**Give a man a fish and you feed him for the day,**
> **Teach a man to fish and you feed him for a lifetime.**'

How can I get that concept across to Eric? He pondered as he made his way back to his office.

Tom gathered the Quality and HACCP manuals from Andrew's office and sat down to read them. After a while, he realised that the route to implementing Roger Connor's vision of Regal Foods becoming a world class food manufacturer and a great place to work lay more in changing the behaviour and attitudes of people like Eric, than in developing better documented quality systems.

Perhaps Walter may have some ideas, he thought. He decided to award himself an early night and headed back to the hotel.

Chapter 4

Day 2 – Evening

The journey back to the hotel was quick and uneventful. As he pulled into the car park, Tom was already starting to wonder what insights Walter could provide on the best way to build a relationship with Eric.

The little bell above the door jangled as he opened it and Richard soon appeared from the kitchen.

"Evening Tom, have you had a good day?"

"Oh yes" said Tom. "So much to think about and digest; I think I will get changed and go for a quick walk before dinner. What time does Walter usually get back? We plan to eat together this evening. It's really fortunate that we met, I suspect I can learn a lot from his experiences."

"I'm sure you will. Walter and I have had many an interesting conversation of an evening when it's been quiet. Although most of his time is spent working with organisations, many of the approaches he uses really help outside work. He introduced me to the DISC model and helped me work out the behavioural styles of my two teenagers. I had always tried to treat them both alike until Walter took me through DISC and I suddenly realised that what worked for one was a real turn off for the other and vice versa. I wish I had known about it sooner. I am sure it would have saved us all a lot of grief! Have you come across DISC?"

"No" Tom replied, "From what you say, it might help me find a way to build a relationship with one of my new colleagues who has a reputation for being difficult."

"Walter normally gets back about six thirty to seven, so I shall expect you down for dinner around seven thirty.

"Thanks. Can we have the table in the window please? I really like the view."

With that Tom went upstairs, showered and changed and then went out for a walk. Back at the hotel, he found Walter sitting at the bar enjoying a gin and tonic.

"Can I tempt you?" Walter queried.

"I would love a lager; I have developed quite a thirst on my walk."

Tom pulled up a stool and sat alongside Walter.

"How's day two been?" Walter enquired with a smile.

"Challenging. Some things better than others. Andrew seems to have made great progress with updating the HACCP schedules and Ian wants me to be involved with developing the new line. I am really encouraged by their open approaches to sharing information and their willingness to involve guys on the shop floor at the very early stages. However, Eric, the works manager, is another case altogether. He still seems locked in a mindset in which he thinks he has all the answers and if only everybody did what he told them there would be no problems! I was hoping that you might be able to give me some pointers as to how best to deal with him."

"I'd be delighted to help in any way I can" replied Walter. "It sounds as if Eric is exhibiting classic high D behaviour."

"Is that anything to do with the DISC model that Richard was telling me about?"

"It certainly is. I first came across this about ten years ago and I was immediately struck by its power and simplicity. I have experienced many psychometrics in the past, both as a candidate and as a recruiter, but I have never found another diagnostic that offers so many valuable insights from so little time needed to complete the DISC questionnaire. Irrespective of whether I am working with senior directors or junior staff, everybody seems to get new insights about themselves or other people close to them."

Tom was intrigued. "Tell me more. What does DISC stand for?"

"Well" said Walter, "let's start at the beginning. The idea of being able to classify our behaviour styles into four categories predates Hippocrates. He came up with a four vector model in 400 BC which corresponds pretty well with the DISC model. DISC came from the work of Dr William Moulton Marston, a lecturer at Harvard who published a book in 1928 called "Emotions of Normal People". This is not a particularly PC title by today's standards, but it was a real breakthrough in understanding people. He wrote that human behaviour could be explained, and hence understood, by observing how an individual initiates or responds to the key concepts of pace and priority. In other words, do they prefer a faster pace or a slower pace, do they prefer to focus on tasks or people."

With that, Walter got out his pad from his briefcase and started drawing. "If we put task at the top of the circle and people at the bottom, then faster pace on the right hand side and slower pace on the left hand side we have the basic framework for defining the components of the DISC model.

Dominance
Influence
Steadiness
Compliance

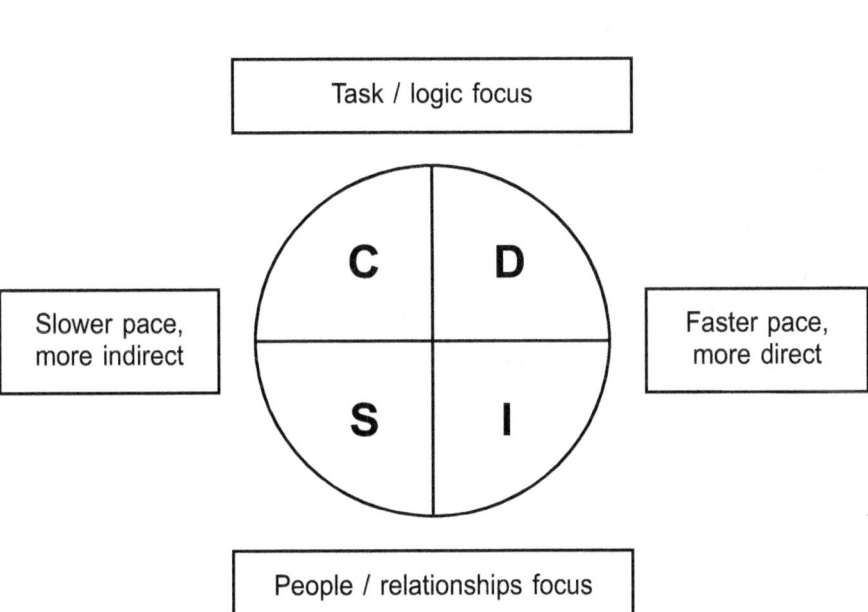

We can see that people who like a faster pace and have a task focus have the **D** as their predominant style and adjectives such as **Dominant, Directive, Determined, Demanding** and **Decisive** all apply.

People with a high **D** in their style are happiest when they are in control, making decisions and achieving results. They can be blunt at times and will openly challenge anything or anyone they disagree with.

If we move round to people who still like a faster pace, but focus more on people and relationships, then the **I** becomes the predominant style and we can use adjectives such as **Inspiring, Imaginative, Impulsive, Interacting** and **Impressionable** to describe their style.

People with a high **I** in their style are much more motivated by recognition and enjoy the company of others, they often come across as open, friendly and trusting and enjoy exploring new ideas.

Staying with the people focus, but moving round to the **S**, people with a high **S** style are often described as **Supporting, Steadying, Systematic** and **Sensitive**.

Such styles thrive on appreciation and tend to accommodate others rather than be in conflict. They work well in teams and like to complete any job they undertake. They are also good listeners.

If we now switch from people to task focus, but stay with the slower pace, we get the **C** style. People with a high **C** style are likely to be described as **Cautious, Careful, Conscientious, Conforming** and **Critical**.

High **C** styles want to know the facts and are most comfortable when they are able to follow well defined procedures. They tend to be logical and well organised but may come across as cool and aloof."

"That's absolutely fascinating" said Tom, "I can already identify that Eric has a high **D** style."

"That's great, but don't forget," Walter cautioned, "that:

> **DISC is best used to help build understanding, not to label or judge. No one style is universally better than another, just different. Each style has its strengths and struggles.**"

"Let's carry on the discussion over dinner. I'm hungry."

With that they made their way into the dining room and sure enough Richard had reserved them the table in the window.

Richard came in and brought them the menus. "What do you fancy tonight, gentlemen? The salmon is as good as ever, the sea bass is fresh today and the wild duck is excellent."

Decisions, decisions, decisions thought Tom; I am really going to enjoy staying here for a few weeks.

"I shall have the duck" Walter decided. Tom dithered and then went for the duck as well.

"How do you get to recognise and understand the different styles?" Tom enquired.

"Well, DISC can best be thought of as the language of behaviour. You have to learn the fundamentals and then it's practise, practise, practise to build your fluency. When you start learning, it can often be useful to think of possible archetypes that are well known. Once you associate a character with a particular style it can help if you recall some of the characteristics of that style.

So Tom, let's take the **D** first. It is possibly the easiest style to recognise as you have already recognised that Eric probably has a high **D** in his style. If you think about the adjectives used to describe the **D** style, who springs to mind? Remember the high **D** style tends to have a strong sense of right and wrong. If you agree with them you are right, if you disagree, you are wrong! They tend to project strong self-confidence and tend only to listen to information that they feel will be of use to them. There is no point trying to get close to them and talking socially unless they are in the mood at that moment."

Tom thought for a moment and said "How about Margaret Thatcher or Alan Sugar?"

"Spot on" said Walter, "but remember most people have more than one factor driving their style and we only see the public persona. Their actual style might be quite different in private."

"What about the high I style with their easy going verbal skills, their persuasiveness, their ability to enthuse others and their optimistic approach to life?"

"I see some of that in me" replied Tom, "but perhaps not to the same degree as Sir Alan showed the **D** on TV in 'The Apprentice'."

"Sure" replied Walter. "As I said earlier, our behavioural style is often a mix of two or three factors which may be only mildly above the line or right at the extreme."

"Can you explain more please, what do you mean by above the line?"

"Well," said Walter taking out his pad again and drawing a diagram. "The version of DISC I use plots the responses to the DISC questionnaire on two graphs to give both your natural style and your adapted style.

The closer to the top or the bottom you are on the graph, the easier it is to observe the characteristics of the high or low style."

If these were the graphs for Eric, then you would easily be able to see the high **D** and low **C** behaviour but might have more of a problem working out where his I and S were.

However, we digress. Let's continue to explore the basic characteristics of each style before we get into more detailed understanding of what the model can tell us.

So who do you think typifies the high I style?"

Tom thought for a moment and then said "Bill Clinton or Tony Blair."

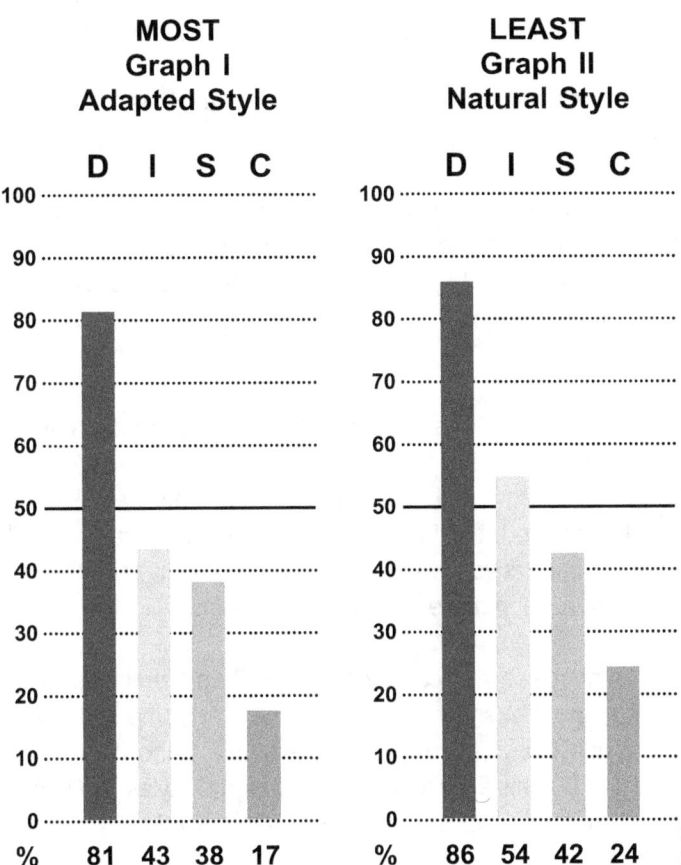

MOST Graph I Adapted Style	LEAST Graph II Natural Style
D I S C	**D I S C**
% 81 43 38 17	**% 86 54 42 24**

"Exactly, both seek to use their charm and verbal skills to persuade and will try to talk their way out of tricky situations! You are really getting the hang of this.

"So what about the high **S** style? This is more difficult to observe and we often use the absence of strong evidence of the other styles to characterise it," Walter cautioned.

Tom thought quietly for a moment and then said "Give me some more clues; I am stumped at the moment."

"Think of a national leader who has a more measured approach than Tony Blair and does not as openly challenge others as Margaret Thatcher did."

Tom went back into thinking mode and eventually suggested, "Nelson Mandela or the Queen."

"Exactly" replied Walter. "Remember, they can be just as passionate about their beliefs as the high **D** and **I** styles, they just express it in a much quieter way. In teams, people with high **S** styles may often be wrongly judged to be less committed than the high **D** and **I** styles as they don't display their feelings so openly.

What about a high **C** style? As with the high **S** they are more difficult to spot in public life. Remember the high **C** styles will be very task focussed and show a high attention to detail. They will probably come across as cool and detached and uncomfortable in social situations with strangers. They may also be seen as indecisive as they seek to gather all the information they need to be confident about the decisions they make."

Walter could almost see the cogs whirring in Tom's brain as he sought to come up with a good example. In the end, Walter came to his rescue and said "I tend to use Gordon Brown as an example, although I suspect there is a fair amount of **D** in his style too. Not many high **C** styles rise to prominence in public life; they tend to function better in support roles."

Richard suddenly arrived with the duck and Walter put away his pad. "Enough of that for the time being; let's enjoy the meal."

They started to eat the meal in silence before Tom's curiosity got the better of him. "So, we have identified Eric as probably having a high **D** in his style. How does that help me build an effective working relationship with him?"

"Two main ways" replied Walter. "Firstly, for each core style there are ways of communicating which help you get your point across and ways which will hinder your ability to get the other person to see your point of view. Take a moment and think about the sort of people that you find it easy to talk to and with whom it seems easy to exchange ideas and information. Also, think about someone with whom you had to work really hard to communicate with. Has anyone come to mind yet?"

Tom thought for a moment and then said, "Well, I always find it much easier to talk to my Mum than my Dad, but I thought that was just a normal mother - son relationship."

"Now you are beginning to understand the DISC model. Using that diagram I drew in the bar, where would you place your Mum and Dad?"

"Well, my Mum was always the more outgoing of my parents and she loved to chat. Talk to anyone she would! My Dad was much quieter and would often spend time with his head in a magazine or a book. He's an accountant who specialises in tax and he is forever reading journals and books on tax law. I suppose I would tend to put Mum in the **I** quadrant and Dad in the **C**."

"Great" said Walter putting down his knife and fork. He picked up his pen and pad and started drawing two pairs of circles.

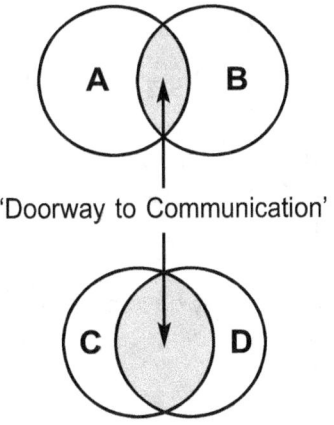

'Doorway to Communication'

"*A* and *B* represent people with very different behavioural styles and *C* and *D* represent people those with similar behavioural styles. We can see that the area of overlap, the 'Doorway to Communication', is much wider open between *C* and *D* than it is between *A* and *B*. In such circumstances, information can flow much more easily and misunderstandings are less likely. Imagine you are talking to someone in the next room and the door is wide open so that you can not only hear them better but also see how they are reacting to what you are saying. The chance of them understanding what you are seeking to communicate is very much higher than if the door is only slightly open and you cannot see their responses."

Tom nodded, "I can certainly see that" he responded.

Walter carried on and started to modify the first pair of circles. "Imagine that *A* understands exactly how *B* likes to be communicated with and flexes their style to meet *B*'s needs. When this happens, the doorway opens and the quality of communication is dramatically enhanced."

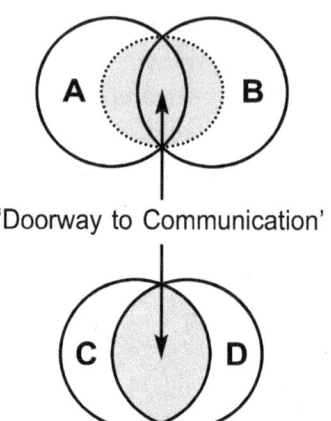

'Doorway to Communication'

Walter carried on, "Remember when you were growing up. Were you ever told that the **golden** rule of communication was to speak to others as you would like to be spoken to?"

Tom nodded. "That works well if they have a similar style to your own," Walter continued, "however, if they don't you could frustrate the hell out of them!

Well, we now have the **platinum** rule for effective communication:

> **Speak to others in the way in which THEY like to be spoken to, not the way in which YOU like to be spoken to!"**

"Now I see why I always found it so much easier to talk to Mum," Tom said with feeling. "We both have similar styles, whereas Dad's is opposite!"

"Exactly" Walter confirmed, "so to communicate with Eric you need to flex your approach to meet his style."

"How do you do that?"

"By learning the language of DISC" Walter replied with a smile. "Each behavioural style has ways of communicating that work better than others. Indeed, the ways that work for one style often completely turn off someone with the opposite style. For the high **D** style such as Eric, the simplest strategy is *be brief, be bright and be gone*! Always focus on results that interest him and never approach him without having your options well thought out beforehand."

"I see" Tom replied thoughtfully, "where can I find out more about DISC and communication?"

"There's a great book by Jim Carey called 'Getting to Know You'[1] which helps you learn to recognise the different styles and develop strategies to get the best out of your relationships, both within and outside work. Unfortunately it is out of print but a colleague of mine ships them over from the US as he has made it essential reading on his leadership course. I have a spare copy in the car that you are very welcome to borrow."

"Yes, please." Tom replied enthusiastically, "I will have a browse tonight."

Walter got up and went out to his car leaving Tom deep in thought.

Walter soon returned, book in hand.

"Here we are, see what you think of it, I can always get you a copy if you want one."

Tom turned to Walter, "Thank you so much for your time this evening - it has been really interesting and valuable. I am starting to realise how important it is to work on my communication skills."

Walter nodded, "From both my personal experience and my reading,

> **it is apparent that the higher up the organisation you rise, the more important your ability to communicate and build effective relationships becomes.**

Which company would you rather work for; one with a leader who is technically one of the best in his field but does not communicate well and cannot retain staff, or one where the leader is technically competent, attracts and retains great people and is known inside and outside the company for his people skills?

"No contest!" Tom said with passion. "I can see I have a lot to learn. I am glad to say that what little I know about our MD would appear to suggest that he communicates well. The article about his vision for the company as being not only the best technically but also a great place to work certainly influenced my decision to apply for this job."

"I did say there were two ways which could help you build a good relationship with Eric. Perhaps we had better leave the other one until tomorrow. It's getting late and I can see you are eager to get started on the book. I have an early start in the morning so will miss breakfast but I will be back tomorrow night about the same time. Sleep well." Walter folded his napkin and got up from the table.

"I will try" Tom replied, "but my brain is buzzing at the moment. I am really fascinated by all this behavioural stuff. I look forward to part two tomorrow!"

Chapter 5

Day 3

Tom got up and had breakfast alone, glad of the opportunity to reflect upon his conversation of the night before and the insights from reading 'Getting to know you'. Although he had only just been introduced to the DISC model it was already starting to make sense and he set himself the task of seeking to identify Andrew's style. Not as easy as identifying Eric's style he thought, Andrew seems much quieter and less outgoing.

He drove into the factory in silence, his mind still trying to identify the aspects of Andrew's behaviour that would identify his style. He soon arrived at Security, signed himself in and parked the car in front of the office block. He noticed Ian's car was already there, so he took the opportunity to check in with Ian before he walked over to his office.

Ian's door was open so he popped his head round the corner. "Morning Ian" he said cheerily, "what's the challenge for today?"

"You tell me" Ian responded with a smile, "How are you getting on with Andrew and our quality systems? Also how did your meeting with Eric go?"

"I had a useful session with Andrew, exploring the HACCP system; he certainly seems to have the key elements well covered."

"He certainly does," Ian agreed. "Once Andrew has been set a task he is very thorough in his approach and has a good eye for detail. However, I have found that he needs regular reassurance that what he is doing is correct. I was rather hoping that you would take over the lead role in the HACCP team from me. I need to free up time to focus on the new production area and you will have a better understanding of the technical issues. I think the first meeting to review the issues for the patisserie line is next Wednesday. I will start it and then hand over to you."

Tom was delighted to have such an early opportunity to influence the way in which the HACCP scheme for the new production line was going to be developed.

"I did not manage to sit down with Eric yesterday afternoon, we just started and then there was a problem on one of the production lines so he dashed off to fix it."

"That's par for the course. Eric does enjoy being in the thick of it. Unfortunately, some of his supervisors now stand back and let him do it. I am still trying to get across to Eric that he doesn't do himself any good, nor does he help the development of the supervisors, by constantly giving them **his** solutions!"

Tom smiled to himself. Classic high **D** behaviour, no solution is ever as good as the one thought of by the high **D** boss.

"I will have another go this afternoon; I recognise how important it is for technical and production to be able to work together effectively. I will let you know how I get on." With that, Tom set off to his office to meet Andrew.

Andrew was sitting at his desk with a worried look on his face.

"Morning Andrew, what's up?" enquired Tom.

"We have just had this email from our seasoning supplier saying there has been a national alert for possible contamination of chilli powder from India with Sudan Red dye. We use their chilli powder in the Hot and Spicy quiche that we produce for Saint Marcus. I was just going through all the other recipes to make sure that we don't use it in any other products."

"Right," said Tom, "let's put aside what we were going to talk about and use this as a practical exercise to test our traceability and product recall systems. You carry on checking out the recipes and I will go and see Eric and get the production records for the Hot and Spicy quiches."

Tom set off down the corridor to Eric's office at a brisk pace.

"Morning Eric. We have a potential problem - some of the chilli powder that we use may be contaminated with an illegal dye which is toxic. At the moment, we think it is only the Hot and Spicy range for Saint Marcus that is affected; Andrew is checking all the other recipes to see whether any other products use it. I need to find out when we produced them and get the batch records for that day."

"No problem," responded Eric. "Fortunately we have computerised our production records, so I can search the database." With that he typed in 'Saint Marcus Hot and Spicy' and a list of dates and quantities came up on the screen. "How far do you want to go back?" he asked.

"Given the short shelf life, we should be OK with the last three months. Or do you freeze any for repacking later?"

"Only in the run up to Christmas" Eric replied, "but we haven't started that yet."

"That's a relief" said Andrew, "how do I get hold of the batch records for those days?"

"They are still held in admin because we are trialling a real time traceability system at the moment. However, it is not totally reliable yet, so we have been running both for the last couple of months."

"Thanks for your help Eric, much appreciated" Tom said as he went out of the office, printout in hand, to retrieve the batch records from admin.

Working his way through the filing cabinet he was greatly reassured to find the records present for all the dates he wanted. He copied them and put the originals back in the filing cabinet, then went back to Andrew's office.

"Got them" he exclaimed, "how are you doing?"

"My memory was accurate; the chilli powder was only used in the Hot and Spicy." Andrew responded: "We have had a further email from our spice supplier to say that the suspect chilli had a batch code 22407P and was only supplied in the last three months."

"Great, where do you keep your raw material intake records? Will they give us the supplier codes?"

"We have an intake book in the laboratory where we log all the ingredients coming on site. That will also give us the batch codes." Andrew got up and went to get the book. Together they scanned the pages and found that there had only been one delivery of 10kg a month ago and it did indeed have the suspect batch code.

"We don't use much" explained Andrew, "the recipe only calls for 50g per batch and it is not a high volume line."

"So, we have only got to check the batch records for the last month to see whether any mix used that code."

"Yes" replied Andrew, "and as a back-up we can go to the raw material store and check the stock of the chilli powder. I will take a quarantine label with us."

According to the batch records, all the chilli powder used had a different code to that suspected of contamination. So they set off for the raw material store hoping to find the recent delivery untouched.

"That's a relief" Andrew exclaimed as they identified an unopened 10kg drum of chilli powder. He completed the quarantine label and stuck it on the drum.

"Celebration time! Let's go for an early lunch and review what we need to do next." Tom continued, "I have been really impressed by what I have seen of your systems. They seem very well disciplined and robust."

"It hasn't always been like that" explained Andrew. "When I first came here, record sheets were often not fully completed and on occasions vital records would go missing. I had to put in a system of checking all the sheets before they were filed each day and often had to go and retrieve sheets from the factory. I took the opportunity to talk with the individuals concerned and explain why it was so important and gradually things got a lot better. There's still an occasional missing sheet, but we catch it the next day and can usually locate it."

Tom nodded knowingly, "I've had the same experience. It's important to have systems, but people need to understand the point of them. I always remember my first boss's advice:

Identifying a problem is easy.
Designing a procedure to overcome it is a little more difficult.
Having that procedure consistently followed six months down
the line is the most difficult of all!

"Wise advice" agreed Andrew. "Our internal audit system has helped, but we do struggle to keep to schedules. Everyone always claims pressure of work to delay carrying out the audit, or they carry out the audit and the action points aren't closed off."

Tom nodded in agreement, "I had exactly the same problem. Back to the problem in hand, what else do we need to do?"

Andrew thought for a moment. "We know that we have not used any of the contaminated chilli powder so we do not have any product at risk and we have isolated the affected ingredient. We will need to contact the supplier to find out when they can replace it and check how long our good stock will last."

"Absolutely," agreed Tom, "is there anything else we need to do?"

Andrew thought for a moment and then said "I guess we should contact Saint Marcus and tell them."

"That would be good. It is always better to take the lead and keep them informed rather than wait until they come chasing you. What else?" Tom enquired.

Andrew looked perplexed.

"It would be good to tell Ian and Eric. Although the problem is potentially sorted, it always pays to keep your colleagues advised, in case they get asked questions.

We could also write this up as a test on our traceability system as it could be useful when we are next audited." Tom explained.

They got up and cleared away their plates and headed back to their offices.

The sun was shining so Tom decided to go and explore the outside of the site. Good exercise and time to think about how best to approach Eric, he reflected quietly to himself.

As he walked around the perimeter road he thought back to his conversation with Eric. He had been brief and to the point and focussed upon resolving the problem and Eric had responded in exactly the way that Tom would have wished. How can I build upon that this afternoon he wondered? Then he realised that there was a chapter in 'Getting to Know You' on the strengths and struggles of the high **D** style. It would certainly pay to review that before he had his meeting with Eric.

Tom made his way back to his office, got out the book and started reading. There were many aha moments as he reviewed the chapters on each of the basic styles. It was all starting to make sense. As he became more confident with his grasp of the characteristics of the four styles he realised that most people often exhibited behaviours that were a mixture of more than one style. He recognised that although he could identify closest with the **I** style, there was more than a little **D** in his approach, particularly if he felt under pressure.

He looked at his watch, noticing it was nearly three. I will call Eric and check when would be best to go and see him. Tom remembered from his reading that an individual with a high D style likes to be in control, so he would let Eric set the time and location. He dialled Eric's number.

"Afternoon Eric" Tom said cheerily. "When would be a good time to get together this afternoon? . . . You're free now . . . OK, your place or mine?. . . I'll be along in a few minutes". With that, Tom got up, collected his pad and pen and set off. He smiled to himself as he recalled reading that high I's can often get so engrossed in discussions that they forget what action points have been agreed. He had realised some time ago that his effectiveness really improved when he wrote down key points and reviewed them later. A simple concept, but not always easy to maintain!

He soon arrived at Eric's office, knocked on the door and went in. Eric was on the telephone and gestured for Tom to sit down. The chair was arranged directly opposite Eric. Tom smiled inwardly as he remembered that the high **D** and **C** styles preferred across the desk conversations, while the high **I**'s and **S**'s were more comfortable with side by side arrangements.

Eric quickly finished his call and turned to Tom, fixing his gaze upon him. "Welcome to Regal Foods" he said. "Tell me how you are going to sort out your staff. They are always trying to tell me what I can't do."

Tom was initially surprised by this very direct challenge and thought for a moment about the best way to respond. "Can you help me understand the problem with some specific examples?" Tom remembered that when challenged by a high **D** it was important not to deny or defend but to stay in problem solving mode.

"Only last week they . . ." Eric fired back.

Again Tom resisted the urge to challenge Eric and stayed calm. "Do you have any other examples?" he questioned. "The more I understand the circumstances surrounding the conflicts the better able I will be to work out how to overcome a situation that you obviously find very frustrating.

Tom continued in this vein for some time, gathering more and more information. Soon a pattern began to emerge. Conflicts tended to happen when there was a shortfall between what was due to be shipped and stock available and Eric was seeking to use stock that had been quarantined for one reason or another. It was the traditional battle between QA wanting to adhere to procedures and specifications and production wanting to get goods out the door.

The discussion went backwards and forwards for some time. As more and more incidents came to light it became clear to Tom that Eric tended to see everything in black and white. If you agreed with him you were right, if you didn't you were wrong!

Tom recognised that he was not going to change Eric's perspective on the behaviour of QA during this discussion and decided to bring it to a halt on as positive a note as possible.

"Thank you for giving me so much information. Obviously I still have a lot to learn about how things work around here and I will discuss the points you have raised with Andrew. Let's meet again at the start of next week when I should have a better idea as to how we might make progress" he said as he made his exit.

"Fifteen all!" he said to himself as he walked back to his office. On the plus side, he had not allowed Eric to intimidate him, nor had he fed Eric's obvious frustration with the behaviour of the QA team. Neither had he said anything which was likely to change Eric's perspective as to the role of QA. Perhaps Walter's forthcoming communication tip might be helpful he wondered as he sat back at his desk and reviewed the events of the day.

Chapter 6

Day 3 – Evening

Walter was already ensconced in the bar when Tom got back to the hotel. "Good day?" he enquired.

"Interesting" responded Tom. "The DISC model certainly helped me understand Eric better, but I still feel we see the world quite differently. His view of the role of QA is, I fear, quite different to mine."

"Let me get you a drink and we can retire to the comfy seats in the corner. I have a suspicion that the other model I was going to introduce you to last night might be of more help in this situation. What would you like?"

"A glass of Merlot would go down exceptionally well, purely for health reasons you understand. I once saw an article which said that half a bottle of red wine in the evening stops you waking up with a heart attack in the morning. I've been trying to get it on prescription ever since, but no luck so far!"

Walter laughed. "When you find a willing GP let me know and I will register too!"

They sat down in the corner. "Tell me exactly how your conversation with Eric went."

"Well, I remembered your advice to be brief and bright, to keep focussed on solutions and not to be intimidated by his direct manner. I also watched his body language. He had a very direct gaze when he was engaged with what I was saying but I noticed his eyes rolled up if I was taking too long to make a point."

"Well noticed" Walter complimented Tom, "the eyes are a real giveaway for the high D. As soon as their eyes roll up, their mind is already elsewhere thinking about something other than your conversation. If that happens, stop talking and ask for his or her opinion about the subject to get them re-engaged. From the sounds of it you were doing a good job at flexing your style to suit his but were still not happy with the outcome."

"That's true" responded Tom. "We just seemed to be seeing the role of QA from very different perspectives."

"Absolutely right, you can use DISC to open up communication channels with colleagues, but if they have very different values there will still be conflict. In such circumstances you will find this model most helpful." With that, Walter took out his pen and began to draw.

He drew a triangle with five layers and then labelled them, starting at the bottom with "Environment". Then "Behaviour", "Capabilities", "Beliefs", "Identity" culminating in "Purpose" above the apex of the triangle.

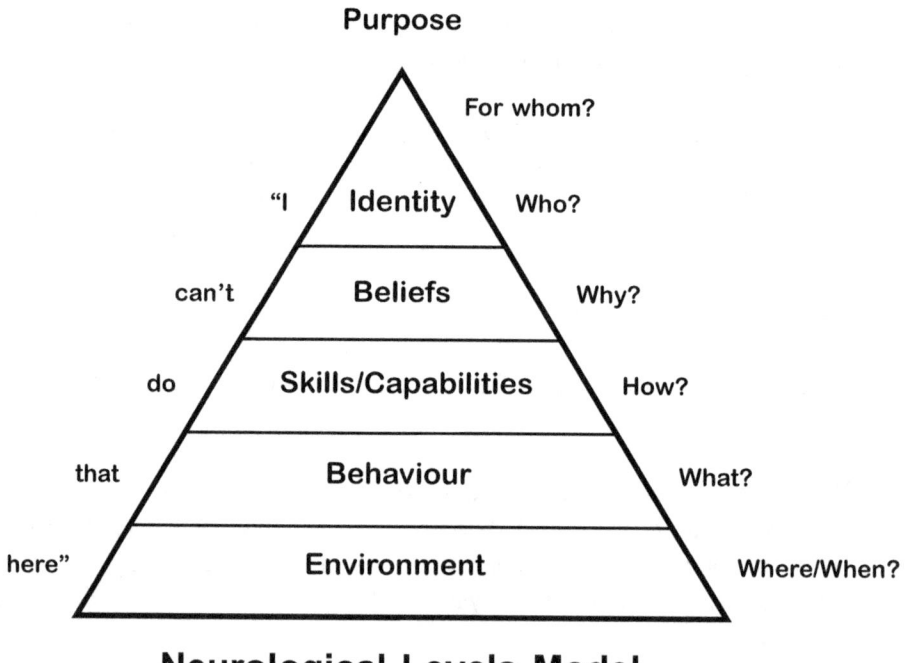

Neurological Levels Model

He went on to explain: "This is a great model for helping individuals and organisations change. I first came across it in a book by Robert Dilts[1] who apparently developed it from the original work of Gregory Bateson, an anthropologist who identified that there are natural hierarchies in the way in which we think, speak and organise our lives. Each level helps to create, order and direct the interactions below it. A change in one of the upper levels would cause a change in the levels below, while a change in one of the lower levels could, but would not necessarily, cause a change in the one above."

Seeing a perplexed look on Tom's face, Walter carried on "Don't worry, it took me some time to get my mind around it but now I have it has really become one of the most valuable tools in my toolkit. Let me give you an example. If someone said to you 'I am not an organised person', do you think providing them with more filing cabinets would help?"

Tom shook his head.

"Do you think sending him on a time management course would help?"

Tom thought for a moment and then said "Probably not."

"Exactly," replied Walter. "If you listen carefully to the exact wording of that statement you will detect that the person concerned does not see themselves as, or believe themselves to be organised (Identity / beliefs). In such circumstances, providing more filing cabinets, i.e. changing the environment is not likely to change their behaviour.

Sending them on a training course could enhance their skills but rarely is problem behaviour down to a lack of skill. It is much more often to do with an individual's beliefs and values or their sense of identity. Once they start believing that they can be organised and start thinking of themselves as an organised person then their behaviour will change.

One of the biggest lessons I have learned over the years of helping individuals and organisations develop is that:

> **Knowledge is very rarely the limiting factor for performance;**
> **it is what an individual does with that knowledge that makes**
> **the difference!**

Tom smiled. "What you are saying is that to get Eric to stop being so critical of my QA team I have to work on his beliefs rather than our procedures."

"Exactly" replied Walter, "Unless there are some real stupidities in your procedures, refining them is unlikely to change Eric's view of QA. It is also probably true that Eric has a reasonable grasp of how the procedures work, so running workshops or other forms of training are also unlikely to have much impact. The change will come when Eric develops a more positive belief about the role of QA in the organisation."

Tom look quizzical "How do I do that?"

Walter began to draw a vertical arrow on his diagram, labelled 'abstract' at the top and 'concrete' at the bottom. He explained, "As you go up to the top of the models, the levels become more abstract, whereas at the bottom, the levels are more concrete or specific. The more abstract the subject the easier it is to get agreement. The more specific, the greater the opportunity for dissent.

For example, if you ask Eric if he believes producing a quality product is important to the company's future, he will readily agree. However, if you ask him whether a particular borderline product should be sent out or reworked, you are much more likely to get into an argument."

"So how do you suggest I approach Eric?"

"Choose your time," Walter replied "Wait for a moment when Eric is more relaxed and start to gently question him about what he believes are the key success factors for the company. No doubt quality will come into the conversation at some point and you can then explore what quality means to him. As you get agreement on the broader issues, gently become more specific and work down the levels, exploring the skills required to be an effective quality manager. Then find out what are the typical behaviours he expects or dislikes before moving on to his views on your current procedures. If at any stage you have a different perspective from Eric, go back up again to the more abstract levels where you were in agreement and examine how each of your perspectives align with the agreed belief or value. In that way you will build upon your areas of agreement.

Sometimes you will find it useful to identify a 'bridge' between differing values. For example, if you identify one of your key values as being recognised as a leading quality producer of quiches and Eric says that being the most efficient producer of quiches is one of his then the bridging value might be the concept of seeking to do 'everything right first time'. Sometimes you will need to have two or three bridging values in order to get agreement.

A smile of recognition lit up Tom's face. "Now, I see," he said "**by developing shared values we can reduce the conflicts** that we are likely to have over quality issues."

"Indeed" responded Walter, "the same model can also help any feedback you give to be more effective in changing your colleague's behaviour. Make sure in your language that you specifically challenge the behaviour instead of questioning the sense of identity of the person you are talking to."

> **Neurological levels separate the deed from the person – you are not your behaviour!**

"Do you have children?" Walter enquired.

"Not yet" Tom replied with a smile, "I am hoping that this job provides the opportunity to settle down and start a family."

"You will find much of what we have discussed will help you get the best from your children when they do arrive. I can remember being picked up by a friend for calling my son daft, rather than saying that what he **did** was daft. It stuck in my mind long before I came across this model."

Walter looked down at his watch, "its way past my bedtime and I have an early start in the morning. Many thanks for your company; I really enjoy sharing my experiences with someone so open to learning."

"It's me who should be so grateful" replied Tom, "I now feel I am much more aware of how to influence people."

Walter smiled and said "I shall leave you with one final thought:

> **Understanding the concept is often easy. Working out what it means to you can be a little more difficult. Consistently embodying it in your behaviour is a lifetime's journey!"**

Chapter 7

Day 4

Tom was up early the next day as he was due to go and visit the factory that produced all the fresh vegetable components for the quiches. This time he remembered to take his notebook so that he could jot down any areas of particular interest to review later.

Tom took advantage of the quiet country roads to give him time to reflect upon his experiences of the previous day. It had really begun to dawn upon him that his ability to really make a difference to Regal Foods was going to be down more to his influencing skills than his technical expertise.

As he approached the factory he wondered whether the way the driver was dressed on Monday was an accurate reflection of the operating standards of the unit. Driving through the gate, his first impressions did little to quell his concerns. The factory appeared to have been constructed out of a series of small individual units around a central yard which had obviously been added to over the years. The empty wooden potato crates stacked up at the entrance did not create the best impression; especially as he could see from a distance that some were desperately in need of repair. He parked in front of the portacabin labelled office and went inside. "Good morning, I'm Tom King and I am here to see Jim Grant."

The lady smiled and said "Please wait here and I will go and get him." A few moments later Jim appeared, red in the face and covered in mud. "Sorry lad" said Jim, "one of the bearings on the peeler is shot and it's a ****** to change. Let me go and wash my hands and then we can have a chat."

A few minutes later Jim took Tom into his office. "Pull up a chair and I will order us a tea. How do you like yours?" While Jim was ordering the tea, Tom took the opportunity to have a look around the office; there was a desk in one corner covered in paper and a couple of pictures on the wall. Jim pushed the papers to one side to make room for the tea. "Bloody paperwork, gets in the way of everything! I keep telling Ian it's pallets out the door not paper that makes the profit," Jim said with passion.

"Ever since we were taken over by Regal it's been change this, change that, more paperwork than I have ever seen in my life and for what? I've had so many visits from people from head office who claim they are here to help me, but all I end up with is more work and hassle! They seem to want to change everything at once and don't realise I have a factory to run."

Tom could sense that Jim was in full flow and chose to let him talk.

"I've been running this place for the last fifteen years and I am bloody proud of what we produce and the service that we provide. Many a morning I have been in at five to start the peelers and have still been here at nine at night. Now all I get is calls telling me that I haven't completed this bit of paper or followed that procedure. Nobody seems to appreciate how much effort goes into getting all the orders out, especially as they keep changing. Your plant in particular has a habit of coming on at four o'clock wanting more diced onions for the next morning."

Tom was listening with one part of his brain while the other was trying to work out how best to build a relationship with Jim. From Jim's point of view he obviously hadn't seen many benefits from all the changes associated with the company's new ownership.

Tom recognised that Jim was displaying many of the characteristics of a high **D** style and remembered that it would be better to seek to solve some of the gripes rather than try and talk socially.

"I can see you have had a frustrating time with some of the changes" Tom started, "I only started here this week, so I am still trying to get my head round the quality and planning systems currently in use. Who looks after your quality procedures here?"

"Florence" Jim replied, "she's been with me since I started and has learnt the job as she has gone along."

"Well, if you are happy to let me spend some time with Florence then I will be able to get some understanding of what you do and perhaps we can make some of the procedures more user-friendly."

Tom remembered the maxim of "be brief, be bright and be gone" as the way to communicate with the high **D** style and quickly finished off his tea.

"Follow me" said Jim opening the door, "let's go and find Florence."

Florence was working in a small office across the yard which had been fitted out as a test area with a cooker and sink, as well as a desk and filing cabinet.

Florence welcomed him warmly and invited him to pull up a stool. Tom explained his new role and they soon got chatting about their past experiences. Tom found Florence very easy to talk to. She told him about the takeover and the changes that had followed.

Right from the start she had sensed that Ian and Jim had very different ways of looking at the world and mannerisms. "I found Ian quite easy to talk to. He seemed to know what he wanted but didn't go shouting about it as Jim is prone to do," she explained. "Also, Ian insisted Jim create me this work area. Before, I just had an old Portacabin as Jim didn't see the point of spending money on anything other than production equipment."

"The downside is that there has been a lot more paperwork since the takeover which we sometimes struggle to complete. Each week, Andrew seems to send us another procedure that we have to follow, and they don't always make sense. At times I feel overwhelmed by it all."

Remembering what he had learnt last night, Tom decided to explore what Florence's perspective was on the role of QA before he got down to the detail of the procedures.

An hour quickly passed as they discussed the role of QA and he was pleased that Florence recognised the importance of documentation of both procedures and results. She appreciated the fundamental element of any quality system:

Do what you say and say what you do.

Tom helped tease out her understanding of the role of QA and the difference between Quality Assurance and Quality Control and was pleased that, in spite of her lack of formal training, she shared similar perspectives with him about the role of QA. He introduced her to four key questions of any quality system:[1]

Can we make it OK? - the capability of getting it right first time.

Are we making it OK? – maintaining control over the process.

Have we made it OK? – does the finished product meet the agreed tolerances for defects?

Could we make it better? – process improvement to enhance perceived quality or lower cost while maintaining quality.

"Can you give me an example of a procedure that doesn't seem to make sense to you?"

Florence thought for a while and then said, "I'm not sure about the point of the one which says that we should only source from approved suppliers. Jim has been in the vegetable business for years and has built up relationships with many growers who have served us well."

"Let's explore what the procedure requires," replied Tom. "It says that you have to use approved suppliers, not that you have to stop using your existing supplier, providing they satisfy an approval process. Which of the questions do you think it addresses?"

Florence thought for a while and then said tentatively, "the first one."

"Exactly" agreed Tom, "if you use a supplier who has their own quality systems, you are much less likely to get defective raw material which could prevent you from getting it right first time. What else?"

Florence was silent for a few moments and then said "could it be to do with pesticide residues?"

"Spot on! Everyone is much more sensitive about pesticide residues and as you know, testing is very expensive and it would not be viable to test each batch produced. By using approved suppliers who have accurate control and documentation of their pesticide usage we can be confident that our products answer the third question – have we made it OK with respect to pesticide residues?"

Florence smiled, "Now I see the purpose of that document. It's not just another restriction on the way we work."

"As documents or procedures come to mind that you can't see the sense of, put them to one side and we will review them on my next visit. If they don't enhance the quality of your operation we will modify them until they do. Remember, they must all meet our maxim of do what you say and say what you do."

Tom recognised the importance of building an open, solution focussed relationship with Florence. Although she reported directly to Jim, she had a dotted line relationship to Tom. Given the physical distance, much of the communication would be by email and telephone, so he knew how important it was to start to build trust in their relationship. He recalled the mnemonic SEEKER, as a guide for building trust, from one of the early leadership programmes he had been on and mentally checked through each item.

Show you understand the needs of the group/person

Establish the guiding principles of how you'll operate

Explain the resources you'll use in this work

Keep to the principles you've elaborated

Engage in constant, honest, two-way communication

Reinforce through consistent behaviours

He was still deep in thought when Jim walked though the door. "Fancy a bite to eat?" he enquired, "we often use the Sportsman in the village. It's usually quiet at lunchtimes and they do good food with the best vegetables for miles around – couldn't get any fresher. We take them some each day."

Tom readily agreed, hoping that a more relaxed setting would provide a good opportunity to get to know Jim better.

Almost as an afterthought, Jim invited Florence to join them.

"No thanks" she replied with a smile, "I will stay here and hold the fort. You go and relax and I will make sure that everything is ready for the three o' clock delivery."

Tom followed Jim back to his office. "I will go and change," he announced, "won't be long."

Tom looked around and saw some aerial photographs of the site; they had obviously been taken some years before, given the styles of the cars and vans. He was still looking at them when Jim came in.

"How long ago were these taken?"

"About ten years" Jim replied, "we had been up and running for about five years, started off in one unit then expanded into another two. Now we occupy the whole site. I will give you a tour after lunch"

"That would be great. The more I get a feel for the operation, the more I will be able to help Florence develop and implement the most appropriate systems."

"The Sportsman's only ten minutes away, do you fancy walking?"

"Absolutely, let's enjoy the sunshine while we can," Tom responded enthusiastically.

Jim regaled Tom with the history of the company. He had started it from the ashes of a previous company with just a small peeler in a shed on his farm with the prepared vegetables being delivered in a trailer attached to his car. After six months they had moved onto the current site and bought a van.

"Couldn't do that now" he said with feeling, "there are so many bloody rules and regulations and people telling me what I can't do – it's a wonder any new business gets off the ground. I got out of farming because of the interference, but now food manufacturing is a damn sight worse."

Tom let Jim talk. The more he could understand how Jim made sense of his world, the more he would be able to find common ground in the debates they would no doubt have over the challenges of building a world class food manufacturing company.

Tom got a real sense over lunch of the resentment that Jim felt over the 'interference' he had had to endure since the takeover.

"I just don't feel that my knowledge and experience is properly valued any more" he complained. "I've been growing and processing vegetables all my life."

Tom listened sympathetically. "The demands of being a food processor are certainly greater now" he agreed, "the challenge is to create the systems that meet our legal responsibilities and satisfy our customers while helping us get the best out of our people and processes. I do believe it can be done, though I must admit I haven't always got it right. I would really appreciate the opportunity to work with you and Florence to take a critical look at the way in which we operate and see if we can develop some better systems that will improve our control while reducing the bureaucracy."

"I'll drink to that" said Jim with a grin.

Lunch was soon over and they made their way back to the factory in the warm autumn sunshine. Tom let Jim do most of the talking, keen to gain an understanding of Jim's beliefs and values. It became very clear that Jim was the key driver behind all activity in the factory. At one point, Jim openly bemoaned the fact that if he didn't do it, it didn't get done!

 "Why is it that no one thinks for themselves anymore?" he complained. The thought crossed Tom's mind that maybe Jim's confrontational style had knocked the confidence of the staff, but he wasn't sure it would be helpful to express that directly at this stage.

They were soon back at the factory. Tom noticed pallets of raw material and finished products sitting out in the sun.

"How many times have I got to tell the forklift driver to put the carrots in the chill as soon as they arrive and not pull out the pallets for delivery until the van is ready?" Jim said in an exasperated voice. Come into the office and grab a coat, hat and wellies and I will show you round."

"That would be really useful," replied Tom, "I have never been round a vegetable processing factory before."

"Let's start with the raw material chill, we only built it three years ago and already it is too small" Jim explained as he pulled open the big door. Tom looked inside and could see pallets stacked three high. "How do you manage with stock rotation?" Tom enquired.

"Can be difficult, it's better now we have our intake labelling system working well, but we can still sometimes miss a pallet."

Tom made a mental note to check the integrity of the traceability system. Jim pulled the door shut and led Tom off into the onion peeling area. Tom's eyes immediately began to water with the fumes. Jim looked at him and laughed." Don't worry, it happens to everyone. Pop back outside into the fresh air for a few moments and then come back in."

Tom did as suggested and upon his return was much better able to see what was going on. The machines appeared new and quite sophisticated. Jim stopped one and showed Tom how it worked. Tom could just about make out what Jim was saying over the noise of the other machines.

"We damn near went bust because of these," Jim explained once they were outside. "The bank got jittery with loaning us half a million pounds to buy them, that's why I agreed to sell out to Regal."

Tom could now better understand why Jim was so sensitive to some of the changes. High **D** styles tend to have a well defined sense of right and wrong. Their ideas are right and other people's are wrong if they do not coincide! He would have to proceed gently if he was going to get Jim to buy into the changes that were already starting to formulate in Tom's mind.

Tom had seen sufficient to appreciate that some of the ways of working reflected more of Jim's agricultural background than was now regarded as good practice for food manufacturing. He realised that unless he could get

Jim to emotionally buy into the new standards he would have a real uphill struggle to tighten up the operating disciplines.

The rest of the afternoon disappeared in a blur as Jim took him round all the different processing areas. He hadn't realised how much work went into producing prepared vegetables. There appeared to be much more complexity than he expected, with many of the vegetables being produced from varying varieties, with differing dice sizes, slice thicknesses and pack weights. It would certainly be a challenge to ensure the QA system covered all the potential variables without becoming so complex that it would be viewed as unworkable. The operating standards were also very different to that of Regal, with wood and cardboard much in evidence and people having to cross the yard to get to different processing areas. As he had anticipated, the environment was not conducive to easy maintenance of good food manufacturing practice. He felt sure he would have many 'interesting' discussions with Jim about how to bring operating practices into line.

Tom said his goodbyes and decided to go straight back to the hotel. Walter had said he would be there by six and Tom wanted to discuss today's experiences.

Tom took the opportunity on his way home to reflect on his conversations with Florence, to gain a better understanding of her style. She had certainly been open and friendly, but in a quiet and measured way, and did not seem to be as focussed as Andrew on the procedural elements of the job. I guess that puts the **I** and the **S** above the **C**, with probably the **S** the highest of them all, Tom reflected. He made a mental note not to try and introduce too many changes at once, remembering how individuals with a high **S** style tended to baulk at rapid change but would not always say so openly. I must go gently and ask for her opinions directly to ensure she understands what we are seeking to do and gets on board. I don't want to go away from my visits thinking she is happy about everything and then discover she has deep reservations.

He smiled to himself as he realised he was already benefiting from his understanding of DISC. It will certainly reduce the chances of misunderstandings in the future, he thought to himself. Thank you Walter!

Chapter 8

Day 4 Evening

Tom arrived back at the hotel with his mind still buzzing with thoughts and questions about his experiences at the vegetable factory. He decided to indulge in a long warm bath before dressing and making his way down to the bar.

"Evening Tom" Walter greeted him warmly. "How's your day been?"

"Absolutely fascinating, there is a very different culture there compared to the main site. Jim, the former owner, appears to have built the business almost single-handed and its farming roots are very apparent. Creating a world class food manufacturing culture is going to be a major challenge. Jim is already resistant to many of the changes that have happened since Regal bought him out six months ago."

"That's often the case" said Walter. "I was reading an article on change management last week which quoted that somewhere in excess of 70% of formal change initiatives fail to deliver the benefits that were used to justify starting them."

"Wow! I knew changing organisations could be difficult, but I never guessed it was that difficult." Tom looked really surprised.

"That's not all" Walter continued. "Every time a change programme is judged to have failed, it actually makes the organisation more resistant to any future initiatives."

"I see," said Tom, "so what you are saying is that the more an organisation launches change programmes that don't deliver the expected benefits, the more resistant people become and the less likely future ones are to work. So re-launching programmes that have not yet had a chance to deliver can actually make the situation worse."

"Precisely" Walter agreed. "As I am sure you recognise, organisational change is not optional. The demands of the marketplace are constantly changing and organisations either change or die. There was a quote in the article which really resounded with me.

> **"It's a whole new world out there, with new playing fields, rules, and players. Your choice is to either learn this new game, or continue to be the very best player in a game that is no longer being played."**
>
> *Larry Wilson[1]*

However, there is a lot of research into change management and some good ideas have come out of it to help us understand people's behaviour and how best to facilitate change. Some of the concepts are quite simple to understand, but that does not make them easy to implement!"

Walter pulled out a pad from his briefcase and began to draw. "Have you ever heard of the Kubler Ross curve?" he asked. Tom shook his head.

"Well" said Walter, "it came out of research into people's thoughts when they had suffered the sudden loss of a loved one. It was realised some years ago that this had more general applicability to any situation where an individual had been subject to a significant, imposed change. Let me take you through the thinking and see how much you can tie it back to your own experience."

What they found was that after the initial shock there was often a period of denial or minimisation as we seek to play down the impact of the change. There then follows a period of self doubt and depression as we recognise that the change has happened and we question our ability to deal with it.

If we take the vertical axis to represent performance and the horizontal axis to represent time, we can see that our performance continues to fall until we can accept the change for what it is, let go of the past and start to look forward to the future. As we do so, and start to test out options and work through what this change means for us, our performance tends to rise back up again. Once we have fully accepted the change we can then put our energy into dealing with the challenges of our daily lives.

Kubler Ross Change Curve

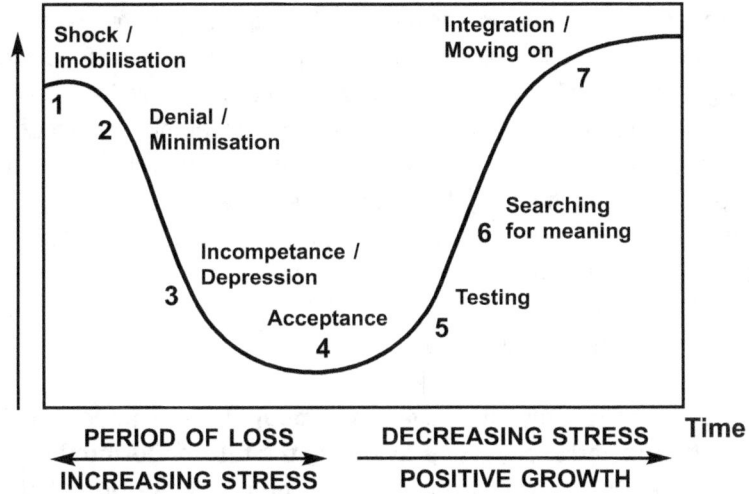

Performance

1 Shock / Imobilisation

2 Denial / Minimisation

3 Incompetance / Depression

4 Acceptance

5 Testing

6 Searching for meaning

7 Integration / Moving on

PERIOD OF LOSS
INCREASING STRESS

DECREASING STRESS
POSITIVE GROWTH

Time

Can you think of a time when you suddenly had to face a major change?"

Tom thought for a moment and then said, "I guess the closest I came to it was when I failed one of my first year exams at university and had to make a decision about whether to stay on doing a course I wasn't enjoying or change to a different course at a different university."

"Can you remember your thoughts at that time?" Walter asked gently.

Tom was quiet for a moment. "I guess I must have followed a similar curve, I certainly did have some time questioning whether university was for me and felt pretty low during that summer. I guess I was well into my second term at the new university before my confidence really came back and I started to enjoy the course."

"Obviously people react to situations differently," Walter continued, "the dip is pretty universal. However, the depth of the dip and the length of time before people recover do vary substantially. There does also seem to be some correlation with behavioural styles, with high **D** and **I** styles tending to be less affected by sudden change than the high **S** or **C** styles. Some people can have a double dip. Just as they start to come to terms with the change, something happens and they go back down into the trough again."

This often happens in organisations where the leadership is not very well skilled in managing change. They spend time planning the change and working through its implications before they announce it. By the time the people at the sharp end are aware of the change, the leadership are already through the dip and well out the other side. They then become frustrated that those charged with implementing the change are not embracing it enthusiastically, so they send them on training courses or, worst of all, write off the first programme as not working and initiate a fresh one.

They don't seem to realise that:

> **training is only effective once people have accepted the change and are starting to look to the future. During the early stages they need supporting and help to work out what the change means for them."**

"Thanks, Walter, now I understand why change is so difficult to manage effectively."

"That was just your starter for ten" Walter interjected with a smile, "there are a lot more concepts I can share with you about managing change. If we have an early dinner, perhaps you would like to adjourn to the bar for the follow up."

"I would really appreciate it, thank you. The very least I can do is put dinner on my tab, I have learned so much from our conversations."

"My pleasure," responded Walter,"always happy to help."

Over dinner, Tom told Walter about his experiences during the day and they explored Jim's attitude towards change. Walter explained that resistance was a normal reaction to change that was being forced upon you.

"How far do you think Jim has accepted the need for change?" Walter enquired.

"Not sure" responded Tom, "Jim recognised the need for financial support, but I suspect he still wants things to be the same as when he owned all the equity and was just a supplier to Regal."

"That's often the case when founders lose control of the businesses they have built. I expect he told you he was too busy to be able to satisfy all the demands of head office. Lack of resources, coupled with a lack of appreciation of the need to change, are frequently given as reasons why a change cannot work"

"How far do you think he understands the thinking behind the new systems?" Walter enquired. "Very often, a lack of understanding of what the new system requires and self consciousness about an ability to grasp new concepts can be real barriers."

"That could well be the case here," responded Tom. "Jim has obviously got great practical knowledge of the products and the processes, but I suspect he left school at a young age to work on the family farm."

"All these factors can conspire to make change more difficult." Walter reached out and picked his pad up from the floor and started drawing again.

"I find this is a useful way to look at the factors that influence change. We call it the change equation."

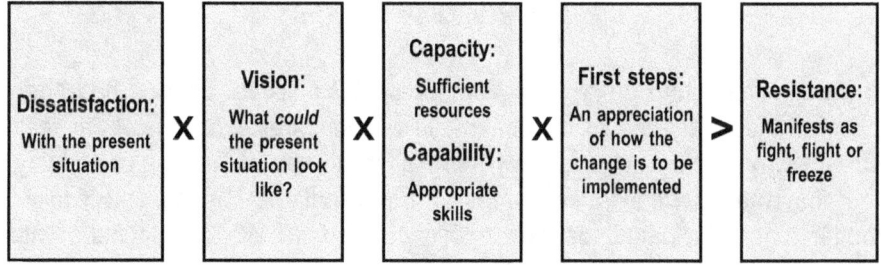

After Beckhard and Harris[2]

Walter turned the pad round so that Tom could read it more easily. "Obviously if any of the factors are zero or negative then the change initiative will not overcome the natural resistance of the organisation."

"I see," said Tom. "What you are saying is that Jim not only has to be able to see the benefits of being part of Regal Foods but he must also recognise the downside of seeking to stay as he is."

"Exactly" replied Walter, "and remember he needs sufficient resources and skills to be able to implement the new systems."

Taking the pad again, Walter drew another graph.

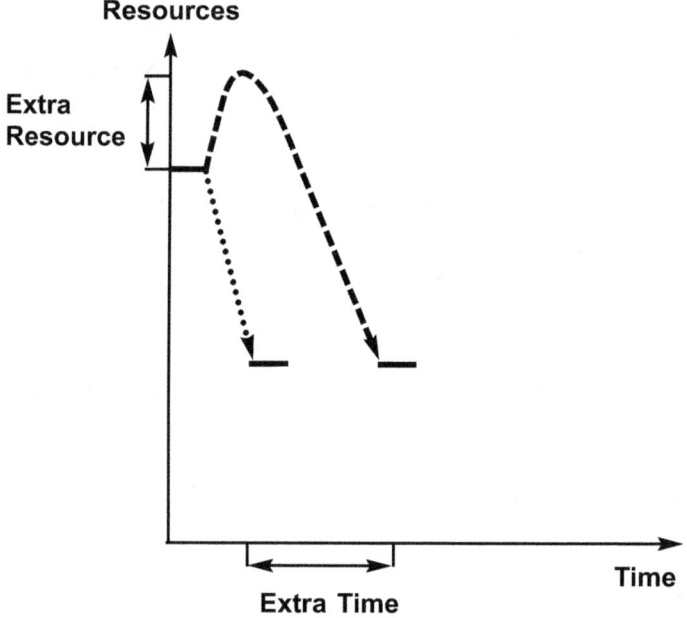

"I have never found an organisation where a significant change has been planned that manages to go directly, in a short space of time, from their current way of working to a new, more efficient way of working. Invariably, they have to invest extra resources to implement the change and it takes longer than anticipated for the benefits to be felt." Walter continued with feeling, "this is particularly true for major IT projects. You have only got to look at the government for examples of projects going way over time and budget. Unfortunately, many leaders are still attracted by the big change projects without being sufficiently aware of the risks and consequences of failure. Major change is much more likely to succeed if it can be broken down into bite size pieces – you have no doubt heard of the saying 'how do you eat an elephant – one slice at a time!' However, more of that after dinner, let's enjoy the meal and I will show you a new tool I have for helping managers understand how best to manage change."

"Thank you. I have a feeling that my ability to implement change is going to be a major factor in my success at Regal Foods," Tom acknowledged gratefully. After dinner, Walter and Tom retired to a corner of the lounge and Walter set up his laptop. He explained that he had recently started to use a simulation to embed the key lessons of how to manage change into the workshops he ran.

"It's called the Change Game[3] he explained, "I first saw it a couple of years ago and became trained to use it. It really has transformed the change module of my leadership programme because it gives my delegates a chance to try out different strategies in a very safe environment. Traditionally, we would explore different change management theories and strategies in a workshop with perhaps a couple of role plays and then the delegates would go back into their organisations and do the real learning on the job, often with disastrous consequences.

As we discussed before dinner, if a change initiative fails it reinforces the resistance to change, often of the whole organisation, because news of failures rarely need communication programmes for the whole world to hear about them!"

"How does the Change Game work?" Tom enquired enthusiastically, "can you show me?"

"Sure," said Walter pulling out a couple of laminated documents from his briefcase. "I split the delegates up into teams of 2 – 4 players, each with a laptop and printer and copies of these laminates. The first is an organisational diagram which shows a multi divisional company with a number of functions in each division and two or three departments in each function. Each department is coloured red, orange or green according to whether the people in it are resistant, reluctant or receptive to change. As you can see, the majority of departments are red, a few are orange and an even smaller number are green."

"Is that normal?" enquired Tom.

"Well, that depends upon the history of the organisation." Walter continued. "In this case, there has been a history of failed change initiatives so not surprisingly only a few areas are still receptive to change. I always ask my delegates to rate their own organisations and the majority are always resistant or reluctant. Very rarely are more than 20 % judged to be receptive. One of the key learning points that come out of the game is to work **with** people receptive to change and work **on** the resistant and the reluctant."

"Now I begin to understand why so many change projects fail. How do you overcome that?" asked Tom.

"That will become clear in time." replied Walter. "Let me give you a little more background to the game, and then you can have a go and find out for yourself. The objective of the game is to introduce new working practices into each of the departments. You can only do this by successfully running projects in that area."

Taking one of the other laminates, he pointed out the first block of options. "You can see that you can run projects in departments, functions, divisions, or even across divisions. The bigger the project the more resources you need and the greater number of rounds you have to play before you get the result."

Pointing to the next block of options he continued, "you can also decide to support a specific project with a range of options such as agreeing outcomes and targets, end user training etc. You also have the option to buy in some extra resources should you choose to do so."

"I remember from that graph that you need extra resources to implement change." Tom interjected.

"Precisely" Walter replied, "and, like real life, if you decide to invest in extra resources you cannot get the benefit of them straight away. You have to wait a couple of periods of play before they become part of your team."

Walter then picked up the remaining laminate and showed Tom a list of 'Environmental' options. "These are activities that you can do to help reduce resistance to change, such as run briefing programmes and workshops for managers and employees."

"Wow!" exclaimed Tom, "how do you know what to do first? There's so much to think about."

"That's the benefit of the game. There is no simple way of ensuring change projects work. You have to work at many levels, using the resources you have to best effect so as to stack the odds in your favour. Let's get started and I will explain more as we go along. First we need to set your team up and give you your initial resources. You start off as the Change Unit Manger with a team of two and 50 TECs."

"What's a TEC?" enquired Tom.

"That's your currency for playing the game. A TEC is a measure of your personal **T**ime and **E**ffort, plus the **C**onfidence the organisation has in your ability to deliver. Every activity you undertake costs you TECs and every successful project pays out in TECs. The TECs also reflect your status within the organisation; if you are successful and earn more TECs than you use then you get promoted to executive and become a director once you have over 100. However, if your projects fail, or you spend more than you get back and your TEC score goes down, you get demoted. If your tally drops below 20, you get relegated to becoming a consultant!"

Tom laughed.

"What's more, the software reflects real life and the more successful you are and the higher your status in the organisation, the easier it becomes to get things done and the actual cost of the activities drops below what is shown on the cards. However, the converse is also true, the lower your status the more the activities cost. In fact, if you have a number of failures and only a few TECs left the chances are the organisation will have become even more resistant to change and the best thing you can do is to look for another job!" Walter said with a smile. "However, that's where this game has the advantage because if you get yourself in that no win situation I can roll back the game to an earlier round and you can then learn from your mistakes and develop a different strategy."

"I bet many organisations wished they had a roll back button." Tom said knowingly. "Let me have a go and see how I get on."

Time flew and it was not until Richard came in and asked if they wanted any more drinks that they realised how late it was.

"I feel more that ready for bed" exclaimed Tom, "it's been a very full day. Thank you so much Walter, as always, I have learned so much this evening. I now need to go and let it all sink in."

"Have this, it's a summary of the key learning points of the game and you will no doubt find it useful to refer back to." Walter handed over a sheet of paper and then packed up his laptop.

"A final thought for you to ponder overnight:

'Ready, Fire, Aim'

Initially, it may seem counterintuitive but it has real significance when it comes to managing major change. I will explain it further in the morning; you will need to be up early as I have to be off by 7.30 to see another client on the way home."

"Thanks again." Tom shook Walter by the hand and they both retired to bed.

Chapter 9

Day 5

Tom's alarm went off at six thirty. It was still dark and the rain was lashing on the window, every reason to stay warm and comfortable for another few minutes. However, he jumped out of bed, not wanting to miss Walter. 'Ready, Fire, Aim' had been running through his brain all night and he was eager to understand its significance. He showered and dressed and went down to the dining room. Walter was already part way through his breakfast as Tom walked over to join him.

"Morning, Tom, you've just made it. I am off in ten minutes." Walter said cheerily.

Tom smiled and sat down. "I'm still not sure of the significance of 'Ready Fire Aim'. Can you explain it more fully please?"

"Sure. Like most management concepts, when you understand the significance it's commonsense. When you don't its divine revelation! I first came across the concept in a book I was reading called Alpha Leadership[1] and I suddenly realised its relevance to the work I was doing helping companies with their change programmes.

Let me ask you a question. If you were an army commander in times of war and you had the option of a battery of large guns or guided missiles and they both had the same explosive power, which would you choose?"

Tom thought for a moment and said, "the guided missiles".

"For what reason?" queried Walter.

"Well, they are more precise."

"Tell me more" Walter encouraged gently.

"If the target moves, they can change course and still hit the target," Tom explained.

"Precisely. If you fire a gun and the target moves you just end up with a very expensive hole in the ground! Now think about the significance for organisations. When companies recognise they need to undergo a significant change, they often spend a lot of time planning the change initiative. They will usually invest significant resources in launching it, with high powered communication programmes, and lots of interest from the senior people. Then what?"

Tom looked quizzically at Walter, willing him to go on.

Walter continued passionately, "not a lot! Often leaders sit back and wait for the results and as we said last night, they are frequently disappointed!

Organisations frequently fail to put in tracking mechanisms to check whether or not the actions they are taking are having the desired effect. It's often not until they realise they have the proverbial empty hole in the ground that they realise their target has moved.

> **In my experience, very few organisations invest in creating sensitive tracking systems so that the leaders know all the time whether their actions are having the desired result.**

Many leaders behave like an airline pilot wanting to fly from London to New York who takes off, heads East and goes and relaxes for a couple of hours before checking his position, finds himself over Iceland, realises he's too far North, so alters course and heads South. Having corrected the error, he then relaxes for a couple more hours before checking position. Now he finds himself over Bermuda and has to turn and head back North East to New York. He then has to hope he can reach his destination before he runs out of fuel.

How confident would you feel if you were on that plane?"

"Not a lot" Tom replied with feeling. "Point taken, I can look back over some of the changes that I have initiated and like that pilot got so far off course before I realised and took corrective action."

Walter looked at his watch. "I must dash. Hope to see you next week and catch up on your progress."

"Thanks again for all your help. I really have learnt a lot this week. Travel safely and enjoy your weekend." Tom said with feeling.

Walter got up and left Tom to finish his breakfast.

Tom drove into work deep in thought, conscious that his first week was coming to an end and mentally checking what he had achieved and what was still important to cover today. He realised that he had not yet talked to all of his team. Certainly, he had spent time with Andrew and Florence and had had a few words with some of the operatives but there were at least a dozen with whom he had not yet spoken. He resolved to catch up with those on the morning and afternoon shift before he left and made the mental commitment to come back in and meet the night shift on Monday evening.

Soon he found himself at the security gate, so he got out of his car, signed himself in and then drove down to the office block. He spotted Ian walking back to his office.

"Morning, Ian" he said cheerily.

"Morning, Tom" Ian replied, "you're just the person I want to see. Can you make sure you are in the training room for 11am? Roger Connor is going to make a webcast and I want all the management team to be present. Will you ask Andrew to attend as well please?"

"Certainly" replied Tom, "what's it all about?"

"Top secret!" Ian replied with a smile. "I don't want to steal his thunder but from what I am getting to know about you, I am sure you will find it interesting."

Tom walked across the yard into his office, took off his jacket and sat down for a minute behind his desk, wanting to jot down his key objectives for the day while they were still fresh in his mind. After a few minutes, Andrew popped his head around the door. "Morning Tom, what's the plan of action for today?"

Tom waved Andrew in. "Good Morning Andrew, it should be an interesting one. The whole management team is to be in the training room at 11 for a webcast from Roger Connor."

"What's it all about?" Andrew asked, with a quizzical and slightly concerned look on his face.

"Ian was being very coy, but he did say it would be interesting, so I don't think there is anything to be concerned about." Tom replied. "No doubt we will have time to discuss it afterwards. Before then, I would like to spend time getting to know the rest of our team. I have said hello to a number of them, but I would like to find out a little bit more. Can you spare some time to take me round and introduce me to them and give me a little background on each one as we go?"

"Certainly," replied Andrew, "if we start about 9.30 they will all have finished their breaks and we should be back well in time for the meeting at 11."

Andrew got up and left. Tom glanced at his watch and saw that he had 20 minutes before going out into the factory. He opened his briefcase and took out the sheet of paper that Walter had given him the previous evening. This may be very relevant to the meeting this morning; he thought to himself and started to read.

The Real Politik of Change
Lessons from the Change Game®

- **Personal Credibility is key**
- **Success breeds success**
- **Work with the responsive (friends and allies initially)**
- **Work on the resistant**
- **Don't work blind**
- **Start in the most promising areas**
- **Load projects for success**
- **Light many fires**

- **Never work uphill**
- **Start with small steps**
- **Communicate, communicate, communicate**
- **Obtain sponsorship and support**
- **Engage with all levels in the organisation**
- **Develop and use the organisation's skills and capabilities**

The first thought that came into Tom's head was that this was not rocket science and he remembered Walter's counselling that it was much easier to understand the concepts than it was to consistently put them into practice! It would certainly provide a useful checklist if he was to be involved in any major change programmes. He was still deep in thought when Andrew reappeared at the doorway.

"Ready?" he enquired.

Tom looked up and smiled. "Sure, let me get kitted up and then we can go meet the team."

The next hour sped by as Andrew went round the factory introducing Tom to all the QA team members. Fortunately, they all had their names on their overalls so learning them was not going to be the usual hurdle. However, Tom wanted to know more about them as individuals, so he got Andrew to give him a potted history of each person they met.

They got up to the training room early and Tom took advantage of the time to be introduced to the remaining members of the management team that he had not already met. Ian arrived a few minutes before eleven and explained that Roger was taking advantage of the new technology so that all of the Regal Foods management team could hear the message simultaneously. It was going to be a relatively short webcast and there would be the opportunity to discuss the implications for their site at the end.

An expectant hush came over the room as the lights were dimmed and the video projector came to life. After a few moments the message "Be the Best" scrolled across the screen and then Roger appeared, flanked by what Tom assumed to be the rest of the Board.

Roger started speaking. "Good morning and thank you for taking time out of your day to listen to my message.

Since I became Group Managing Director at the start of the year, I have been conducting a thorough review of all our operations with the assistance of the Board of Directors. We have come to recognise that in the current economic climate, we are faced with the challenge of producing more, with fewer resources, for customers who demand more for less.

In such a situation, the approaches that we used in the past to build Regal Foods are no longer a guarantee of our future success. As you are aware, we have spoken on many occasions of our objective of making this company renowned not just for its products and service, but also for being a great place to work. We now intend to refine and publicise our mission and the values by which we operate, as a framework by which we will run our business. Whilst we have been very efficient in the way we have run many parts of our business, we have not always been as effective as we could have been in harnessing the talent that we have within the business.

As you can see from the following diagram, the shape of the business will change.

Individual areas of efficiency

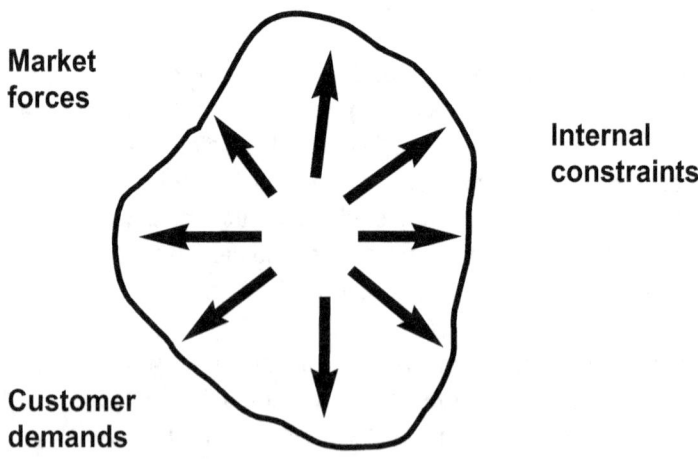

Market forces

Internal constraints

Customer demands

This diagram shows that we may be very efficient in responding to the challenges the business faces, but we are not as effective as we could be. This is because different actions may actually take the company in opposite directions. In the following diagram, by contrast, our sense of mission and the boundaries set by a common set of values ensure that actions taken by all parts of the company help to move the company in the desired direction.

We have invested a considerable amount of time and energy in defining what we believe are appropriate statements of our mission and values. However, these are just a first draft.

Effective use of resources

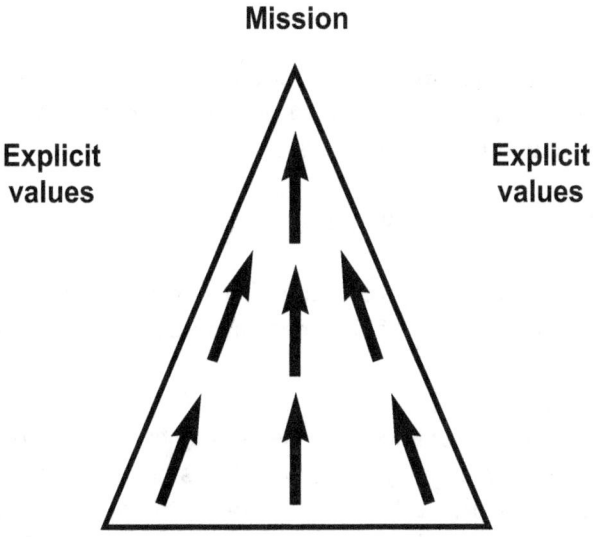

It is essential that all interested parties have an input into the final form of our Mission and Values and I invite all members of our management team to explore and debate the meaning of these statements and feed back their suggestions for changes. Once that phase of the process is over, each manager will be invited to discuss the revised statements with their teams and feedback any further refinements. Key account managers will simultaneously be discussing the statements with our customers.

Whilst the final versions may not be ready until the middle of next year, we would like to start the process of Managing by Values and have provided you all with some weekend reading. Your senior managers will be holding meetings with you over the next few weeks to decide how to maximize the benefit of this approach to our organisation.

Whilst we, the board, have initiated this approach, it is important that all interested parties have the opportunity to participate in their final form, because they will provide the framework by which we run the company in the future.

We have arranged for our initial statements to be printed onto some small cards so that you may easily carry them around with you and use them to help guide your thinking.

Our vision is to be:

> **a constantly evolving organisation where everyone enjoys anticipating and responding to our customers to the mutual benefit of all our stakeholders**

and we have defined our mission as:

> **To be recognised within our industry as the leading company in all we do and to set the standards by which others are judged.**

We have set our sights on becoming the leading company in our industry in the eyes of our customers, suppliers, employees and our competitors. Being good is no longer sufficient. We want to 'Be the Best', hence the name of this programme. The words have been chosen with care. 'Being' involves living and we want every person in this organisation to live the values, not just pay lip service to the concepts.

As will become clear over the coming months, 'Managing by values' is not a quick organizational fix dictated by the board but a way of thinking and behaving in which everybody in the company has a part to play.

We have initially defined our core values as:

- *We will conduct our business with energy, integrity and professionalism in a customer-focused team culture.*

- *We will create an environment which supports continuous learning and innovation with respect to people, product and process.*

- *We will operate to the highest standards of personal health and safety, product safety and respect for the environment.*

- *We believe that long-term relationships are the key to our future and that they must be based upon fairness and mutual benefit.*

I invite all the managers viewing this webcast to set aside some time to discuss these values and explore what they mean to you as individuals and where you see the gaps between our current behaviours, policies and procedures and the values espoused in the 'Be the Best' programme.

Thank you for listening. I look forward to your feedback."

With that, Ian switched off the projector and turned to the group. "First reactions?"

There was an uncomfortable silence for a few moments as everyone digested the message.

Eric was the first to speak. "It's all very well talking about consulting people and involving them, but we don't have time, orders have to be met and sometimes somebody has got to take charge otherwise nothing gets done."

Ian look around the room, "what do other people think?"

Sharon, the accountant, then spoke. "From our figures, we are one of the most profitable sites in the business so I don't see why we need to change."

Tom sat listening and reflecting upon how the 'Be the Best' programme tied in with the concepts he had been exploring with Walter.

He caught Ian's attention. "May I add my perspective?"

"Of course," Ian replied with an encouraging look.

"I know I have only been here a week and I still have so much to learn about this business. If I reflect back over my experiences with my previous companies, I now recognize that all their problems centred on people issues. If this programme helps us all to develop more effective ways of working together then we must all benefit."

Ian nodded in agreement, "I understand some of the concerns that you have all expressed. As Roger said, this is not a quick fix for all of our problems. However, I have the advantage of having read a little about the process and I am convinced that in the long term we will not only be a more productive company but also a much more enjoyable place to work."

Ian reached under the table and pulled up a brown box. "Weekend reading! This book[2] is a great introduction to the process of 'Managing by Values'. I know some of you are already familiar with Ken Blanchard's *One Minute Manager* series so you will recognise the style. It's a quick and easy read and will hopefully stimulate some thoughts as to the implications of using the 'Managing by Values' approach on our site."

Ian passed the books around to all the managers. "If you turn to page 39 you will see a summary of the 'Managing by Values' process:

The MBV Process

Phase 1 : *Clarifying* our mission/
purpose and values

Phase 2 : *Communicating* our
mission and values

Phase 3 : *Aligning* our daily
practices with our
mission and values

I would like us all to focus some time and energy over the next few weeks to gain clarity amongst ourselves as to our mission and values. As Roger indicated, we have some printed reminders which I would like you all to keep with you as both a guide and something to reflect upon in your quieter moments."

There was a chorus of "What are those?" Ian smiled and carried on. "We will meet again next Friday at eleven for a more detailed discussion of our feelings about these statements."

The group broke up and Tom and Andrew made their way back to Tom's office. "I would appreciate some time with you, Andrew, later on this afternoon to get your initial thoughts. Is that OK?"

"It should be fine" Andrew replied, "if we have a walk round just after two. I will introduce you to the members of our crew on the afternoon shift that you haven't yet met and then, barring any crises, we should be able to get some time together."

"Many thanks. That will give me time to tie up a few loose ends. I would like to be away promptly this evening as I have a good couple of hours' drive home."

Tom walked into his office and pulled out his briefcase. At that moment the telephone rang. It was Ian.

"Tom, I have to be away promptly today as I have a function to go to this evening. Can you make yourself free for three thirty for a quick review of your first week? That will enable us both to get away by five."

Tom looked up at the clock and saw it was already after midday. "I was going to meet up with Andrew to share perspectives on Roger's presentation. I will reschedule and come over to you for three thirty."

Tom went to look for Andrew. Fortunately, Andrew was sitting at his desk, busy reading his copy of 'Managing by Values.'

"Andrew, sorry, change of plan. Ian would like to review my first week with him at three thirty, which I suspect will go on to finishing time. I would still like to meet the rest of the staff as planned at two if possible. Could we reschedule our discussions for Monday?"

"No problem, it might even be more beneficial for us both to have read the book. I am only just into the second chapter and already it has got me thinking."

"That's great; I will see you at two."

Tom went back into his office and sat down at his desk. Time to collect my thoughts, he reflected. He pulled out his pad and started to draw a mind map. He had been introduced to the technique on a management development course some years earlier and had found it to be a much more effective way of gathering information together than linear lists; he liked the freedom to add information as it came to him.

"Priority next week, find out who the site tecchie is and get my laptop connected to the site system so that I can print." He muttered to himself as he tore up the first version, silently giving thanks for the software he now used which allowed him to make major alterations and still keep the mind map looking neat and tidy.

Starting afresh, Tom was now satisfied that he had the main topic areas in place and started to expand them a little. As he did so he created a list of all the possible areas for attention that he had noticed on his travels during the week and made the commitment to himself to create a mind map on his laptop when next alone in the hotel.

When he looked up at the clock, Tom saw it was already long after one thirty. Oops! I had best grab something to eat otherwise it is going to be a long, hungry journey home, he thought. He jumped up and made his way to the canteen which was deserted except for the two ladies behind the counter. Tom bought a sandwich and a cup of tea and made his way over to a table in the corner. Suddenly the door burst open and in bounded Eric.

"What's left Sheila?" he enquired, "I'm hungry and I have only got ten minutes before my next meeting."

"Just as well, we saved you a dinner" she replied kindly.

Eric took the plate, grabbed a knife and fork and headed in Tom's direction.

"Come and join me, I'm tight on time too."

Eric sat down opposite Tom and started to eat.

"What did you think of the webcast this morning?" Tom enquired gently.

"Not convinced" Eric replied between mouthfuls, "I am all for getting people to work more effectively together, but they need strong leadership from someone who is willing to take charge and make things happen."

Tom smiled inwardly as he recognized Eric's enthusiasm for the command and control style of leadership. He thought carefully before replying, recognising that this was neither the time nor the place to openly confront Eric's perspective.

> **"Strong leadership is certainly essential if we are to become the best. From my experience and from my reading of history the most powerful leaders really engaged emotionally with the people they were leading."**

Tom could see a flicker of consternation in Eric's eyes as he struggled to work out whether Tom was agreeing or disagreeing with him.

"Must go, I am meeting all the supervisors at shift change; no doubt we will have more discussions next week." Eric got up and shot out of the door.

Tom sat quietly for a moment, reflecting on the exchange. Another draw, he thought. It is certainly going to be an interesting challenge to get Eric to really buy into change in leadership style necessary to really implement the 'Be the Best' philosophy.

Tom cleared the plates and walked back over to his office to meet Andrew.

"Ready?" Tom enquired, "to take me round to meet the troops? Next week it should be safe to let me out on my own!"

Andrew laughed and they set off to the changing room. The atmosphere was good humoured as they went around and Tom was delighted to observe what

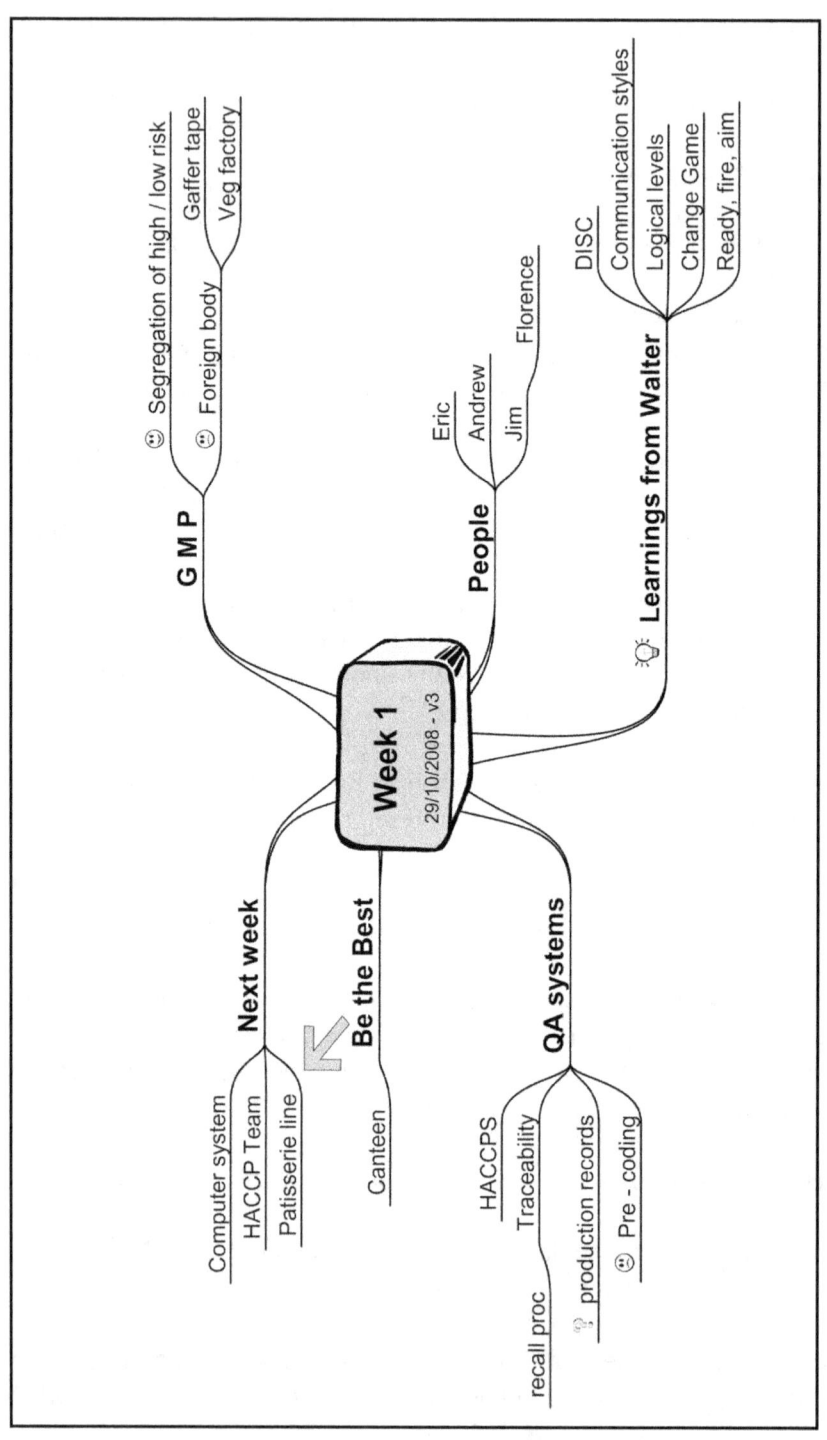

Mind map created using MindManager software

an open relationship he had with all the staff. Behind the gentle teasing there was obvious respect. Tom was reassured that Andrew's style was naturally more in tune with building an empowered team than was Eric's. Tom was conscious of time and had to cut a few conversations short in order to ensure he was ready to see Ian at 3.30.

"Thanks Andrew, you have been a great help and I have really enjoyed this week. I am sure we are going to be able to work well together - you have created some good foundations upon which we can build."

"My pleasure Tom and I hope your review with Ian goes well. Have a safe journey home." Andrew left Tom to collect his briefcase and make his way across to Ian's office.

Tom knocked on the door and went in.

"Take a seat Tom. Would you like tea or coffee?"

"Tea would be great." Tom replied as he carefully chose the chair at right angles to Ian, wanting to create the best environment for an open discussion.

"How's this week been for you?" Ian enquired gently.

"Fascinating, challenging and demanding. So much to take in, so much to do, I don't think there is any danger of me being bored here."

Ian laughed. "I'm sure there isn't, particularly if we add implementing the 'Be the Best' programme to the rest of our challenges. What have been your key discoveries?"

Tom took a folder out of his briefcase and selected the mind map. "I took the opportunity to make a few notes after your call. Would you like me to talk you through them?"

"Yes please."

Tom glanced down at his mind map. "If we start with the technical side, my general impression is that the standards of good manufacturing practice are generally well observed. In particular, the separation of high and low risk operations and the personal hygiene standards. From a foreign body perspective, the sieving of powdered ingredients is obviously very beneficial, but there is more to do in some areas with temporary engineering. I think we have a much bigger challenge with the vegetable processing factory. Not only are there intrinsically more hazards but I am not so sure how much that team understand, or are committed to, the GMP standards that we require."

Ian nodded. "I know we have a challenge with Jim and his team, but I was hoping that now you are on board we can give them more support."

"I think this is important. I got the impression from Jim that whilst his financial worries have eased since the takeover, operational demands have increased, particularly with the paperwork. I have offered to work with Florence to ensure that the systems we introduce are tailored to their environment and don't make unrealistic demands upon their skills and resources."

"What else have you discovered?"

"Well, staying with the technical side, I think that Andrew has done a good job with many of the systems. The HACCP schemes are well documented, if a little cumbersome, and I have agreed to work with him to explore ways of simplifying them and getting more people involved in the process."

"As we discussed, I will be handing over leadership of the HACCP team to you next week. I look forward to seeing the results."

Tom continued, "I am a little concerned by attitudes to pre coding. I know it can be a common practice in the industry to fudge around the edges of date code changes, but this undermines the integrity of the whole quality system."

Ian thought for a moment before replying. "I think you will find the problem disappears as we start to implement the 'Be the Best' programme. One of the key processes of managing by values is to identify the gaps between current practices and the values espoused. I think even Eric would have trouble aligning that practice with our values of integrity and commitment to the highest standards of product quality and safety.

"Perhaps the 'Be the Best' programme will also help get the funding needed to refurbish the canteen."

Ian smiled, "I certainly hope so, and it would be a very visible commitment to everyone on site that we intend to use our value statements to guide our decisions."

"That would also tie in with what I have come to understand is one of the success factors for leading change. I have been very fortunate this week to have the company of Walter at the hotel; he has really opened my eyes to new ways of understanding and influencing people."

"Tell me more about this Walter. From the tone of your voice you seem very enthusiastic about what you have learnt."

Tom continued with passion, "Walter used to run food factories but now specialises in helping companies get the best out of their people. I have learned so much from our discussions over dinner. He's introduced me to so many different concepts, or models to help understanding, as he calls them. I have found them incredibly useful, both to understand why things have worked or not worked in the past and particularly how to build relationships with people that I may have struggled with in the past. I know it's early days but I am now much more confident of my ability to form a productive relationship with Eric, in spite of his views about QA."

"You might share your formula with your colleagues; I am sure some of them back off from challenging Eric at times when it would be beneficial for the company for him to be challenged."

"Have you heard of DISC?"

Ian thought for a moment and then replied, "The name is familiar, I seem to remember the group HR manager referring to it at one of our senior management meetings, but I cannot remember the details."
"I'm still finding out about it myself, but from what Walter has already taught me I have a better understanding of how to relate to styles like Eric's. The phrase 'be brief, be bright and be gone' comes to mind."

Ian laughed heartily. "What else did you learn from Walter?"

"He showed me a number of other models which I think could be really useful in helping us with the 'Be the Best' programme. There was one called 'logical levels' which showed how changes in behaviour could be best achieved by working with people's beliefs and values. He also talked about how important it was for organisations to have their different levels in alignment which ties in well with Roger's diagram on effectiveness. He also showed me the 'Change Game."

"What's that?" Ian queried.

"It's a computer-based simulation whereby you have to change working practices in an organisation where most people are resistant to change."

"I can recognise that," Ian said with feeling. Roger's predecessor launched a big new change programme a few years ago and it didn't work out as we intended. Some people still remind me of it when I talk to them about introducing changes here."

"That's precisely the point of the game; it gives managers a chance to explore different ways of managing change in a safe environment. There's even a roll back button so if it all goes wrong you can turn the clock back and start again."

"I wish we had one here!" Ian said with feeling. "I sense Walter has had a big impact on you. Are you going to be seeing him again?"

"Hopefully next Thursday evening. He is due to stay overnight at the Sportsman and we have arranged to meet for dinner. If you are free, I am sure Walter would be happy for you to join us."

Ian thought for a moment. "That might be a good idea; it sounds as if Walter has a lot of useful experience and with all the changes about to happen here it could be very useful to have him help us. I recall wise advice given to me by my father when I first started driving: 'You can read all about it, you can watch others, but there's no substitute for having an experienced instructor in the passenger seat when you first take the car on the road!'"

Ian glanced down at his watch and then pushed his chair back. "Sorry to cut short this conversation; I must go, I have to be at a meeting at seven and it's a good hour's drive away. Let's meet on Monday morning and review your priorities for the week. Have a safe journey home and welcome to the team; I'm sure you have a lot to contribute."

Tom sat quietly for a moment, finishing his cold cup of tea. He packed his briefcase, got up and walked out of the office to his car.

As he drove out the gates, Tom was conscious of how tired he felt. It had been a demanding week, but fatigue was compensated by a deep seated knowledge that the insights he had acquired into how to influence human behaviour would enable him to really make a difference to food safety at Regal Foods.

Appendices

Appendix 1 – DISC model

1.1 Understanding your own behavioural style

"He who knows others is learned . . . He who knows himself is wise."

Lao Tse

The idea of being able to better understand human behaviour by the use of a four vector model predates Hippocrates. This brief questionnaire enables you to identify the key aspects of your own behavioural style, your preferred mode of communication and begin the journey of understanding others. Within the model, no one style is better than another; each style has its strengths and potential limitations. The more explicitly we understand ourselves and appreciate the similarities and differences of others, the more effective we are in whatever we choose to do.

Directions

Working along each line of the list opposite, identify which behaviour is typically **MOST** characteristic of you and assign 4 points to it, 3 to the next most characteristic, 2 to the next and finally 1 to your **LEAST** characteristic behaviour.

Total your score for each column and transfer it onto the graph (check sum of all 4 columns =80)

D		I		S		C	
Direct		Influencing		Steady		Cautious	
Decisive		Optimistic		Patient		Restrained	
Bold		Enthusiastic		Stabilising		Analytical	
Pioneering		Positive		Willing to please		Respectful	
Forceful		Charming		Easygoing		Curious	
Determined		Convincing		Good natured		Careful	
Restless		Popular		Friendly		Orderly	
Competitive		Talkative		Accomodat-ing		Precise	
Total		**Total**		**Total**		**Total**	

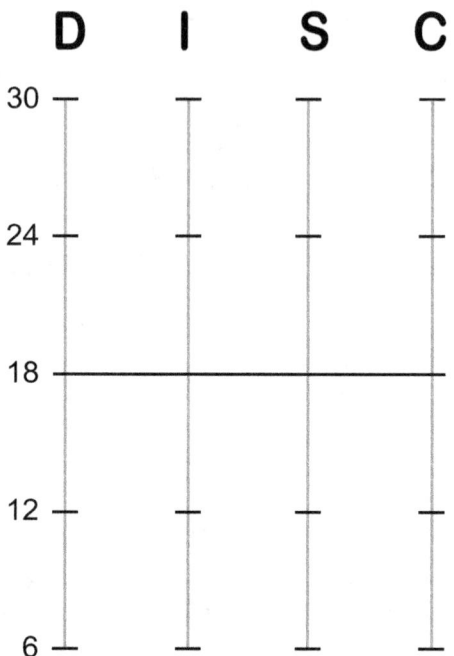

This graph gives you an idea of the behavioural style that you think is most appropriate to succeed or survive in your current role.

For a more detailed analysis of your natural and adapted behavioural style and the associated most effective, and least effective, ways of communicating with you it is necessary to complete a full DISC profiling tool. Target Training International is the world leading provider of DISC based behavioural profiles; sample reports may be downloaded from www.paradigm-partnership.co.uk Please email the author (Adrian) for details about how you may run your own personal report.

1.2 Understanding and communicating with people exhibiting different styles

High D – Eric

Strengths

- Results focussed
- Initiates action – enjoys taking the lead
- Willingness to confront problems
- Outgoing and confident
- Uses 'gut instinct'

Struggles

- Listening to others
- Appreciating the shades of grey
- May overpower others and stifle discussion
- May talk before thinking
- Considering all the possibilities before taking action

Communication tips

- Be brief, bright and to the point
- Don't try to build relationships with social chat unless the other person/people initiate it
- Provide options for action and allow the other person/people to choose
- Don't allow disagreement to become personal, take issue with the facts not the person
- Seek to provide win / win solutions

High I – Tom

Strengths

- Good at building relationships
- Open style engenders trust
- Optimistic and forward looking
- Verbally persuasive
- Solving people problems

Struggles

- May have trouble completing tasks
- Staying organised, utilising time effectively
- May overwhelm others with too many words
- Disciplining others, especially where relationships may be threatened
- May be overly trusting

Communication tips

- Leave time for relating and socialising
- Don't overwhelm with data
- Seek opinions and options
- Don't talk down to them
- Provide ideas for implementing action and document next steps agreed
- Don't waste time exploring "flights of fancy"

High S – Ian

Strengths

- Effective completer of tasks
- Reliable and supportive team player.
- Good listener, can help others achieve their goals.
- Adds stability to the group
- Good at short term planning

Struggles

- May resist imposed change
- May be too accommodating
- Showing their feelings, may be viewed as cool / uncommitted to particular actions
- May procrastinate on decisions when in the leadership role
- May act to avoid risk or confrontation

Communication tips

- Provide a friendly, safe environment
- Don't rush straight to business
- Provide time for people to think through decisions
- Don't promise anything that you cannot deliver
- Allow time for people to ask questions
- Don't be over demanding or adopt a confrontational style

High C – Andrew

Strengths

- Methodical, works well with data and procedures.
- Good problem solver
- Sets high standards for self and others
- Quiet and conscientious, able to work alone
- Follows rules and procedures

Struggles

- Paralysis by analysis
- May be overly critical of self and others
- Building relationships with others, may come across as aloof and cold
- May be slow to act, especially where objective data is scarce
- Taking risks

Communication tips

- Stick to business
- Don't be abrupt, confrontational or rapid
- Challenge with facts and figures, not opinions
- Don't try and force quick decisions
- Provide options and solutions which minimise risk
- Don't invade other people's personal space

Appendix 2 – Food Safety

2.1 Foundation Stones for successful Food Safety Plans

Set out below are what we believe to be the key foundation stones that need addressing when setting up as new, or auditing an existing Food Safety plan or system. They reflect the 'fundamentals' as defined by the BRC in its Global Standard for Food Safety, (see Appendix 4). In addition to the foundations that have been defined, a check list of the key points falling under the various topic headings has been provided. However, this is not intended to be a comprehensive list of food safety issues but rather pointers for anyone involved in food safety. Appendix 4 contains further reading on the technical aspects of food safety which should be referred to for more detail.

1. The senior management of a company must be fully committed to the generally accepted standards of food safety and ensure that adequate and appropriate systems are in place to maintain the company's food safety plan and to correct non-conformity when such actions are identified.

2. The food safety and quality plan of a company must be properly documented and should be based on the principles of HACCP as defined by the *Codex Alimentarius.*

3. A company must have in place an effective and ongoing audit plan to identify non-conformity and systems to record corrective actions.

4. All companies should have a full traceability system and a tried and tested product recall procedure.

5. All premises and plant used for food production should be designed and maintained to prevent, as far as possible, food contamination. In addition, appropriate housekeeping and cleaning regimes should be maintained to ensure consistent standards of hygiene and ensure compliance with any relevant legislation.

6. Provision of facilities and personal protective clothing for staff should be such that they minimise the risk of food contamination.

7. Appropriate and effective pest management systems should be in place in all food production and storage areas of the business.

8. Where raw materials and/or finished products require special handling and separation from others (e.g. allergens), adequate provision should be made to ensure appropriate isolation and this should be clearly documented.

9. All companies should have in place appropriate systems to ensure that they comply with HACCP based food safety plans and that products are safe and legal for their intended purpose.

10. All companies should ensure that staff responsible for producing safe and legal food are demonstrably competent to carry out their function.

2.2 Key considerations for effective food safety

Preventing cross-contamination:

- Cross-contamination, while usually referring to microbiological contaminants, may also be caused by chemicals or insects. Appropriate systems must be developed to prevent problems with any of these.

- Cross-contamination is especially dangerous when the contamination affects products that will not receive any further treatment or processing.

- Means of cross-contamination may be via a variety of vectors including humans, equipment, food surfaces, pests or inappropriate storage (e.g. same refrigerator for raw and cooked products)

- One of the most common vectors of cross-contamination is the hand. The importance of regular and appropriate hand washing, especially after using the toilet, therefore needs to be emphasised.

- There is a need to have physical separation of raw and cooked products in a process facility (e.g. use of ovens as dividers)

- Careful consideration must be given to raw materials as a possible source of contamination in process plants.

Importance of Temperature Control

- Foods need to kept, as far as possible, out of the 'Danger Zone' (usually considered to be 5 to 70°C).

- All cooked products must reach a centre temperature of 70°C.
- All refrigerator and deep freezer temperatures should be regularly checked and recorded.
- Cooking cannot be relied on to remove chemical (including microbial toxin) contamination, thus prevention is the best approach to this potential problem.

Implementing an Effective HACCP System

- The most effective HACCP team comprises all levels of staff.
- An effective HACCP plan requires everyone to be involved from day one.
- Effective implementation of HACCP requires ownership of the plan.
- Education and training must go hand in hand with HACCP implementation.
- It is important to recognise the difference between 'hazard' and 'risk'.

The importance of knowledge transfer techniques

- Formal training needs to be complemented by on the job training / coaching; key knowledge points need to be documented and training records maintained.

Pest Management

- Pest management/control is a legal requirement.
- Pest control prevents product contamination and saves wastage of materials and product.
- A properly managed pest control system eliminates the use of pesticides which might contaminate food.
- Effective pest management prevents structural damage e.g. gnawing of electrical cables.
- There is much advantage in using a specialist pest control company, BUT final responsibility still lies with the food company.
- An effective approach to pest management is DPD (**d**issuade, **p**revent and **d**estroy).

Complying with food legislation – labels, allergies and product recalls

- It is important that the company understands the concept of due diligence

- The importance of ensuring that food labels are correct cannot be over emphasised.

- All staff need to understand the requirements of food allergy control and labelling.

- The company must have and fully appreciate the need for a documented and tested product recall procedure.

- It is a legal requirement to be able to demonstrate full traceability of all ingredients and packaging materials.

- All staff must recognise the consequences of non-compliance with food legislation – and that such action is a criminal offence.

Using customer complaints in a positive information flow system

- It is advantageous to develop a good working relationship with the appropriate enforcement authorities.

- The company needs to recognise the usefulness of negative and positive feedback to measure effectiveness of control systems and identify areas where change is needed.

- It is useful to allow employees to be made aware of customer complaints so that such problems can be avoided in the future.

- Full record keeping of customer complaints is usually a specific requirement under audit systems.

2.3 Common areas of non-compliance

Audits carried out on a range of food manufacturing premises frequently identify the following common non-compliance issues. These should be noted to ensure the company does not fall foul of similar matters.

- Incomplete and non up to date documentation

- Lack of traceability for selected ingredients
- Calibration and verification documentation missing
- Internal audits not carried out or recorded
- Records of clean-down after use of allergenic materials not available
- Minor structural damage to the fabric of buildings left unrepaired (e.g. floors and walls)
- Fraying and damaged conveyor belts still being used
- Equipment found to be rusting
- Metal detectors not regularly checked for compliance with specification
- Foreign objects stored in food production areas (e.g. elastic bands)
- Changing rooms for staff poorly maintained and workwear and outdoor clothing stored together
- Raw waste meat illegally disposed of to land-fill

Everyone involved in the food manufacturing process has a responsibility to ensure that they comply not only with the letter of the requirements for food safety (i.e. HACCP plans, requirements of the Global Standard for Food Safety etc.) but also with the spirit of the requirements. Encouragement by management and a team approach is the only way to achieve the consistent high standards now expected in food manufacture. Often, it is not the lack of technical knowledge that results in problems but more often a lack of communication and understanding about why certain actions or procedures are required.

This Appendix is designed to act as a reminder of some of the technical aspects of Food Safety whereas the purpose of the book has been to stress the importance of communication and the application of knowledge.

It is indeed not what you know but what you do with what you know that truly makes the difference.

Appendix 3 – References

Chapter 1
    1. SMYTHE, JOHN. *The CEO Chief Engagement Officer,* Gower, 2007. p 40

Chapter 4
    1. CAREY, CHRIS. *Getting to Know You,* Creative Communication, Georgia 2001*

Chapter 6
    1. DILTS, ROBERT. *From Coach to Awakener,* Meta Publications, 2003 p299 – 324

Chapter 7
    1. PRICE, FRANK. *Right First Time,* Gower, 1984 p10

Chapter 8
    1. www.larrywilson.com
    2. BECKHARD, R & HARRIS R T, *Organisational Transitions,* Addison Wesley, 1987
    3. ORRIDGE, MARTIN
       www.thelearningcup.com

Chapter 9
    1. DEERING, ANNE; DILTS, ROBERT; RUSSELL JULIAN, *Alpha Leadership,* John Wiley & Sons, Ltd. 2002
    2. BLANCHARD, KEN & O'CONNOR, MICHAEL, *Managing by Values,* Berrett-Koehler Publishers Inc, 1997
    3. www.mindjet.com

Appendix 4 – Further Reading

'Soft Skills'

Alpha Leadership   Deering, Anne; Dilts, Robert; Russell, Julian.
John Wiley & Sons, Ltd. 2002
ISBN 0 470 84483 3

A simple but elegant leadership model bought to life by many examples with practical applications of key concepts.

Managing by Values   Blanchard, Ken & O'Connor, Michael.
Berrett-Koehler Publishers Inc, 1997
ISBN 1 57675 274 7

A readily readable, metaphorical guide to introducing the Managing by Values concept into an organisation.

Getting to Know You   Carey, Chris.
Creative Communication, Georgia 2001*
ISBN 0 9709307 0 4

Practical guide to using the DISC model to enhance your communication skills in a variety of situations both personal and business.

The CEO Chief Engagement Officer   Smythe, John. Gower, 2007
ISBN 0 566 08561 1

Highly readable guide to engaging employees based upon the author's extensive research.

The One Minute Manager series   Blanchard, Ken & others.
Various Publishers

Powerful, practical insights into improving management performance in a variety of contexts.

*Currently out of print but available in the UK from www.paradigm-partnership.co.uk

Food Safety

Managing Food Safety   Engel, D; Mac Donald, D and Nash, C.
Chadwick House Group Ltd 2001
ISBN 1 902423 72 0

*Full of useful and highly relevant technical information which is
presented in a clear and easy to understand style; it is well indexed
and has a good list of follow-up information sources.*

Food Safety for Supervisors   Nash, Claire.
Chartered Institute of Environmental Health (CIEH) 2000
ISBN 1 902423 03 8

*An easy to read introduction to the subject of food safety with practical
advice relevant to those new to the subject.*

Practical Microbiological Risk Analysis   Mitchell, Dr RT.
Chartered Institute of Environmental Health (CIEH)
ISBN 1 902423 4 X

*A useful introduction to the concept of Risk Analysis as a fundamental
methodology underlying the development of food safety standards. The
book has plenty of practical advice and is designed for technical
management staff.*

Hygiene for Management   Sprenger, Richard.
Highfields.co.uk Ltd (Latest edition 2008)
ISBN 1 906404 17 8

*A comprehensive and practical book on all aspects of food safety and
hygiene. This book has been in print (but regularly updated) for many
years and is one of the standard texts in food safety.*

**ISO 22000 Food Safety: Guidance and Workbook for the Food
Manufacturing Industry**   Smith, D; Jackson-Smith, T and Politowski, R.
British Standards Institute (BSI) 2007
ISBN 0 580 49989 0

A practical guide aimed at those in the food manufacturing sector (although guides for other sectors of the food trade are also available) wishing to implement ISO 22000-2005.

Effective Food Hygiene Training   MacAuslan, Euan.
Highfields.co.uk Ltd 2003
ISBN 1 904544 134

Focuses on the practicalities of training but does not contain technical food safety information. This book stresses the importance of competency in food safety matters rather than simply the achievement of certification.

HACCP   Mortimer, S and Wallace, C.
Blackwell Publishers 2004
ISBN 0 63205648 4

A simple guide to the concept of HACCP, it provides the essentials of the topic and is based on a larger work by the same authors. The information is clearly presented and the key points are highlighted. To make understanding easier, there is a series of checklists, flow charts and diagrams.

BRC Global Standard for Food Safety - Interpretation Guideline
TSO (The Stationery Office)
ISBN 0 117025 81 3

The guideline discusses the principles behind each of the requirements clause by clause, assisting companies to effective implementation. A discussion is included on how to prepare for a BRC audit, what to expect during the audit and what actions are required following an audit to maintain certification.

About the Authors

Adrian Banger has over 30 years' experience of food manufacturing in production, technical and general management roles as a manager, director and consultant. Over the last 18 years he has recognised the importance of 'soft skills' in organisational performance and now specialises in helping individuals and organisations harness and develop their intrinsic talents through executive coaching and leadership development workshops.

Adrian is Managing Director of The Paradigm Partnership Ltd, a virtual consultancy which focuses on helping individuals and organisations develop ways of thinking that turn potential into performance. He works with a variety of organisations both in the private and public sectors, at middle manager and board level, facilitating team development and culture change programmes.

He holds a Masters degree in food science and is a qualified coach, NLP trainer and behavioural analyst.

email: asb@paradigm-partnership.co.uk

web: www.paradigm-partnership.co.uk

Philip Barlow is a graduate in both Environmental Health and Food Science and Technology. He originally qualified as an EHO and worked as a food inspector in the UK Local Authority service. Following a move to an academic career, Philip has specialised in food safety and has published c.50 papers in this area. He was until recently the Director of the Food Science and Technology Programme at the National University of Singapore and also a member of the Agri-Veterinary Board of Singapore. After returning to the UK he chaired the Food Standards Agency Task Force on Food Fraud and has now taken up an academic position at the University of Nicosia to assist in the development of a new degree programme in Food and Nutrition. With experience of food safety legislation enforcement, industrial R & D work and food safety education and consultancy activity in the UK and SE Asia, he brings a wealth of scientific and technical knowledge, along with practical experience, to this book.

email: philip0@btinternet.com

Insights

Implications

Intentions

Insights

Implications

Intentions

Insights

Implications

Intentions

Insights

Implications

Intentions

Insights

Implications

Intentions

Insights

Implications

Intentions

Insights

Implications

Intentions

www.ingramcontent.com/pod-product-compliance
Lightning Source LLC
Chambersburg PA
CBHW060631290526
45793CB00001B/213